T0260923

PDF Explained

John Whitington

O'REILLY®

Beijing · Cambridge · Farnham · Köln · Sebastopol · Tokyo

PDF Explained

by John Whitington

Copyright © 2012 John Whitington. All rights reserved.
Printed in the United States of America.

Published by O'Reilly Media, Inc., 1005 Gravenstein Highway North, Sebastopol, CA 95472.

O'Reilly books may be purchased for educational, business, or sales promotional use. Online editions are also available for most titles (*http://my.safaribooksonline.com*). For more information, contact our corporate/institutional sales department: (800) 998-9938 or *corporate@oreilly.com*.

Editor: Simon St.Laurent
Production Editor: Kristen Borg
Proofreader: O'Reilly Production Services

Cover Designer: Karen Montgomery
Interior Designer: David Futato
Illustrator: Robert Romano

Revision History for the First Edition:
2011-11-30   First release
2012-05-23   Second release

See *http://oreilly.com/catalog/errata.csp?isbn=9781449310028* for release details.

ISBN: 978-1-449-31002-8

[LSI]

1338301902

Table of Contents

Preface

The Portable Document Format (PDF) is the world's leading page description language, and the first format equally useful for print and online use.

PDF documents are now almost ubiquitous in the printing industry, in document interchange, and in the online distribution of paginated content. They are, however, widely viewed as opaque and delicate and are poorly understood, even by those of a technical disposition.

This is partly due to a perplexing lack of documentation; the file format reference is freely available, but is of a size and complexity which requires a time investment unlikely to be plausible for the majority of those working with PDF.

This book aims to be an approachable introduction. It is suitable both for the technically minded, and for those who just want to understand a little of the PDF format to give context to their work with tools which produce or process PDF documents.

Who Should Read This Book

We've tried to write a book which serves as a general introduction, with some optional technical interludes, giving you the chance to type in example PDF files and see how they display.

This book is suitable for:

- Adobe Acrobat users who want to understand the reasons behind the facilities it provides, rather than just how to use them. For example: encryption options, trim and crop boxes, and page labels.
- Power users who want to use command-line software to process PDF documents in batches by merging, splitting, and optimizing them.
- Programmers writing code to read, edit, or create PDF files.
- Industry professionals in search, electronic publishing, and printing who want to understand how to use PDF's metadata and workflow features to build coherent systems.

Organization of Contents

Chapter 1, Introduction

In this chapter, we give a history of the PDF format and put it into context. We look at the advantages PDF has over similar technologies, introduce specialized kinds of PDF files such as PDF/X and PDF/A, and take a brief tour of the elements which comprise a typical PDF document. We conclude by looking at how PDF is used in industry.

Chapter 2, Building a Simple PDF

We begin in earnest, building a simple PDF file from scratch in a text editor. We show how to process this into a fully valid PDF and open it in a PDF viewer. We explain each component of the file, taking our first look at various parts of the PDF syntax.

Chapter 3, File Structure

In this chapter, we describe the layout and content of a PDF file, and the syntax of the objects from which it is built. We describe how a PDF document is read from a flat file into a structured format and, conversely, written from that structured format to a flat file.

Chapter 4, Document Structure

In this chapter, we leave behind the bits and bytes of the PDF file, and consider the logical structure of its objects, describing how pages and their resources are arranged into a document.

Chapter 5, Graphics

We describe how to create vector graphics and raster images in PDF, and how to deal with transparency, color spaces, and patterns. We illustrate with examples, showing the code and the result in a PDF viewer.

Chapter 6, Text and Fonts

In this chapter, we look at the PDF operators for building and showing text strings using different fonts and sizes, and how to build lines and paragraphs. We describe the different types of fonts and encodings in PDF documents, and how they are defined and used. We look at the process of text extraction from a PDF document.

Chapter 7, Document Metadata and Navigation

Here, we discuss topics not directly related to the visual appearance of the document, but to ancillary data: bookmarks, metadata, hyperlinks, annotations, and file attachments. For each, we describe how they are defined in PDF and give examples.

Chapter 8, Encrypted Documents

We look at how encryption and document permissions work in PDF, and see how to inspect encryption information in Adobe Reader. We describe how programs which process PDF files read, write, and edit encrypted documents.

Chapter 9, Working with Pdftk
> In this chapter, we show how to use the popular *pdftk* program for the command-line processing of PDF files, looking at common usage scenarios. We describe what a program such as *pdftk* has to do internally to achieve certain tasks (for example, merging or splitting documents).

Chapter 10, PDF Software and Documentation
> Here, we describe both Adobe and open-source software for viewing, converting, editing, and programming with PDF files. We give sources of further documentation and other resources such as support and discussion forums.

Content Updates

May 22, 2012

- Added an index
- Corrections and clarifications to history of PDF in Chapter 1
- Changed references to PDF 1.0 throughout to PDF 1.1, and to PDF 1.5 for transparency related files.
- Fixed an incorrect line ending for OS X/Unix
- Clarified language about string encodings
- Clarified that ID strings should match for newly created PDFs
- Added a comment about cross-reference invalidation

In addition, a few small errors have been corrected throughout the text.

Acknowledgments

I should like to thank my editor, Simon St.Laurent, who was enthusiastic about this project from the beginning. Leonard Rosenthol at Adobe provided valuable comments. Thanks are due to those readers who spotted mistakes in the first release and took the time to contact the author.

Conventions Used in This Book

The following typographical conventions are used in this book:

Italic
> Indicates new terms, URLs, email addresses, filenames, and file extensions.

Constant width

> Used for program listings, as well as within paragraphs to refer to program elements such as variable or function names, databases, data types, environment variables, statements, and keywords.

Constant width bold

> Shows commands or other text that should be typed literally by the user.

Constant width italic

> Shows text that should be replaced with user-supplied values or by values determined by context.

 This icon indicates a warning or caution.

Obtaining Code Examples

All the example PDF files in this book are available for download in a zip archive from the O'Reilly website (*http://oreilly.com/catalog/0636920021483*). The text of the book contains enough information to reconstruct these examples (with the exception of encrypted documents, which are not suitable for typing in manually).

The examples include the PDF source for the figures in this book.

Using Code Examples

This book is here to help you get your job done. In general, you may use the code in this book in your programs and documentation. You do not need to contact us for permission unless you're reproducing a significant portion of the code. For example, writing a program that uses several chunks of code from this book does not require permission. Selling or distributing a CD-ROM of examples from O'Reilly books does require permission. Answering a question by citing this book and quoting example code does not require permission. Incorporating a significant amount of example code from this book into your product's documentation does require permission.

We appreciate, but do not require, attribution. An attribution usually includes the title, author, publisher, and ISBN. For example: "*PDF Explained* by John Whitington (O'Reilly). Copyright 2012 John Whitington, 978-1-449-31002-8."

If you feel your use of code examples falls outside fair use or the permission given above, feel free to contact us at *permissions@oreilly.com*.

Safari® Books Online

 Safari Books Online is an on-demand digital library that lets you easily search over 7,500 technology and creative reference books and videos to find the answers you need quickly.

With a subscription, you can read any page and watch any video from our library online. Read books on your cell phone and mobile devices. Access new titles before they are available for print, and get exclusive access to manuscripts in development and post feedback for the authors. Copy and paste code samples, organize your favorites, download chapters, bookmark key sections, create notes, print out pages, and benefit from tons of other time-saving features.

O'Reilly Media has uploaded this book to the Safari Books Online service. To have full digital access to this book and others on similar topics from O'Reilly and other publishers, sign up for free at *http://my.safaribooksonline.com*.

How to Contact Us

Please address comments and questions concerning this book to the publisher:

O'Reilly Media, Inc.
1005 Gravenstein Highway North
Sebastopol, CA 95472
800-998-9938 (in the United States or Canada)
707-829-0515 (international or local)
707-829-0104 (fax)

We have a web page for this book, where we list errata, examples, and any additional information. You can access this page at:

http://oreil.ly/pdf-explained

To comment or ask technical questions about this book, send email to:

bookquestions@oreilly.com

For more information about our books, courses, conferences, and news, see our website at *http://www.oreilly.com*.

Find us on Facebook: *http://facebook.com/oreilly*

Follow us on Twitter: *http://twitter.com/oreillymedia*

Watch us on YouTube: *http://www.youtube.com/oreillymedia*

CHAPTER 1

Introduction

The Portable Document Format (PDF) is the world's leading language for describing the printed page, and the first one equally suitable for paper and online use. In this chapter, we take a tour of its uses, features, and history. We look at some useful free software and resources, some of which we'll use later in this book.

A Little History

Today we take the high fidelity exchange of documents for granted, knowing that a document sent here will appear the same there and vice versa, and that it may be displayed equally on screen and on paper. This was not always so.

Page Description Languages

We could pass documents between users, and from user to printer, as a series of bitmap pictures (e.g., TIFF or PNG), one for each page. However, this doesn't allow for any structure to be retained, precludes scaling to different paper sizes or resolutions without loss of quality, involves huge file sizes, and so on.

A *page description language* like PDF is a way of describing the contents (text and graphics) of a printed or onscreen page using highly structured data, often with extra *metadata* describing various aspects of the document (such as printing information or textual annotations or how it is to be viewed or printed). This way, decisions about how the document is rasterized (converted to pixels by a printer or on screen) can be left until the end of the production process. A PDF file can contain text and associated font definitions, vector and bitmap graphics, navigation (such as hyperlinks and bookmarks), and interactive forms.

PDF is used wherever the exact presentation of the content is important (for example, for a print advertisement or book). It isn't normally suitable when the content is to be laid out or reflowed at the last moment, such as in a variable width web page—languages like HTML and CSS, which separate content from presentation, are more suitable in those circumstances.

Other page description languages

Many page description languages were created when the printing of lines of text in fixed fonts began to be replaced by digital graphics printing. The printer would then process the language to generate a bitmap at the appropriate resolution. For example, PostScript (Adobe), PCL (Hewlett Packard), and KPDL (Kyocera). Simpler languages were used for vector plotters (for example, HPGL from Hewlett Packard).

These languages varied in complexity and functionality. PostScript files, for example, are full programs—the result of executing the program is the document's visual representation. These languages often contain extra instructions to control aspects of the document other than the page content, for example, which tray paper is drawn from or whether the output is to be duplexed.

Development of PDF

PDF began as an internal project at Adobe to create a platform-neutral method for document interchange. PostScript was already popular in the print community, but wasn't practical for onscreen use with the computers of the day—especially for random access (to render page 50 of a PostScript document, one must process pages 1–49 first). The idea was to use a subset of the PostScript graphics language together with ancillary data to create a structured language for standalone documents to be viewed on (or printed from) any computer.

PDF 1.0 was announced in 1993, with Acrobat Distiller (for creating and editing PDF files) and Acrobat Reader (for viewing only), both as paid-for programs. Later on, Acrobat Reader was made available to everybody at no cost, leading to the widespread use of PDF for the exchange of documents online.

Over the next 10 years, after a slow start as prepress features were added, PDF overtook PostScript as the language of choice in the printing industry. Today, it is the only general page description language of note.

Some Advantages of PDF

When a number of formats compete to be the industry standard, the best contender is not always the victor—luck can intervene. In this case, though, PDF had a number of singular advantages. We look at some of them here.

Random access and linearization

Unlike PostScript, any object (page, graphic, etc.) in a PDF document can be accessed at will, in constant time. This means it's no harder to read page 150 than page 1. *Linearization* is the process of arranging the objects in the file such that all those needed for a given page are located in adjacent positions. This explains why you can quickly jump to any page in a PDF being viewed in Acrobat Reader in a web browser window —the viewer doesn't need to load the whole file to begin with, it fetches from the server just the sections needed to display each new page.

Stream creation and incremental update

Stream creation is the ability inherent in the PDF format to allow files to be created in order, from beginning to end, even if the eventual file is larger than the memory available.

Incremental update means that, when editing a file, it's possible to write the changes to the end of the file without modifying any existing part—this makes saving changed versions very fast, and can be used to provide an undo mechanism (since the previous version is still intact).

Embedded fonts

Fonts used in a PDF are embedded along with the document. This means that it should always be rendered correctly, regardless of which fonts are installed on a given computer. The program creating the PDF document will remove unnecessary data from the font (such as unused characters), so the file does not become unduly large. PDF supports all common font formats, such as TrueType and Type 1.

Searchable text

Most PDF files maintain the information to map the character shapes making up the text to Unicode character codes. This means that you can copy and paste text from a document, or search the text easily. More recent developments in PDF allow the logical order of the text in the document to be stored separately from the layout of the text on the page, preserving yet more structured information.

ISO Standardization

PDF was released as an open standard by the International Organization for Standardization (ISO) in 2008. The ISO-32000-1:2008 document is largely the same as the PDF file format document previously released by Adobe.

This independence lends legitimacy and oversight to the PDF standard, which should encourage its further adoption. However, with no real tools for detecting whether a file meets the standard (Adobe Reader will happily load malformed files, so many tools create them), genuine rigor is some time away.

The PDF File Format Document

The PDF File Format Version 1.7 is documented in ISO 32000-1:2008, which is available on CD or as a PDF for 380 Swiss Francs at the International Organization for Standardization (*http://www.iso.org/iso/catalogue_detail?csnumber=51502*).

The almost identical Adobe Document "Adobe PDF Reference, Sixth Edition, version 1.7" is available in PDF format at the Adobe PDF Technology Center (*http://www.adobe.com/devnet/pdf.html*). Adobe extensions, which do not yet form part of the ISO standard, are published at the same location.

Unfortunately, the PDF File Format is no longer available in print.

Specialized Kinds of PDF

There are several specialized variations on the PDF format—both standardized and in development. These are subsets of the PDF format. Each file is a valid PDF document, but with restrictions on the facilities used or the content itself. Two of these, PDF/A and PDF/X, are now ISO standards.

PDF/A

The PDF/A Standard (ISO 19005-1:2005) defines a set of rules for documents intended for long-term archiving in libraries, national archives, and bureaucracies. It also requires a "conforming reader" to act in certain ways, using the embedded fonts, using color management, and so forth. Briefly, the restrictions on PDF/A are:

- No encryption
- All fonts to be embedded
- Metadata is required
- JavaScript is disallowed
- Color spaces specified in a device independent manner
- No audio or video content

There are two levels of PDF/A compliance: PDF/A-1b ("level B compliance") requires exact visual reproduction of the document. PDF/A-1a ("level A compliance") requires that text can be mapped to Unicode, and that the order and structure of the text is documented, in addition to the requirement of exact visual reproduction.

PDF/X

The PDF/X Standard is a family of ISO standards for graphics exchange in the printing industry, the latest of which is PDF/X-5 (ISO 15930-8:2010).

It defines a number of restrictions:

- All fonts must be embedded
- All image data must be embedded
- Cannot contain sound, films, or non-printable annotations
- No forms
- No JavaScript
- No encryption

and a number of extra requirements:

- The file is marked as PDF/X with the subversion (e.g., PDF/X-5).
- Bleed, trim, and/or art boxes are required, in addition to the normal page size. These boxes define the size of the media, the printable area, the final cut size, and so on.
- A flag is set if the file has been *trapped*. Trapping is the process of creating small overlaps between graphical objects to mask registration problems in multiple color printing processes.
- The file must contain an *output intent*, a color profile describing how it is to be printed.

Version Summary

PDF is fully backward compatible (you can load a PDF version 1.0 document into a program designed for PDF 1.7) and mostly forward compatible (programs written for PDF 1.1 or later can often load PDF 1.7 files). Forward compatibility is ensured because readers ignore content they don't understand—it's only when new compression methods or object storage mechanisms are introduced that this may be broken. Since PDF 1.5 in 2003, such changes have been minimal. PDF versions and their features are summarized in Table 1-1.

Table 1-1. Functionality in PDF versions 1.0 to 1.7 Extension Level 8

PDF version	Acrobat Reader version	Launched	Summary of new features
1.0	1.0	1993	First release.
1.1	2.0	1996	Device independent color spaces, encryption (40-bit), article threads, named destinations, and hyperlinks.
1.2	3.0	1996	AcroForms (interactive forms), films, and sounds, more compression methods, Unicode support.
1.3	4.0	2000	More color spaces, embedded (attached) files, digital signatures, annotations, masked images, gradient fills, logical document structure, prepress support.

PDF version	Acrobat Reader version	Launched	Summary of new features
1.4	5.0	2001	Transparency, 128-bit encryption, better form support, XML metadata streams, tagged PDF, JBIG2 compression.
1.5	6.0	2003	Object streams and cross-reference streams for more compact files, JPEG 2000 support, XFA forms, public-key encryption, custom encryption methods, optional content groups.
1.6	7.0	2004	OpenType fonts, 3D content, AES encryption, new color spaces.
1.7 (later ISO 32000-1:2008)	8.0	2006	XFA 2.4, new kinds of string, extensions to public-key architecture.
1.7 Extension Level 3	9.0	2008	256-bit AES encryption.
1.7 Extension Level 5	9.1	2009	XFA 3.0.
1.7 Extension Level 8	X	2011	Not yet known.

What's in a PDF?

A typical PDF file contains many thousands of objects, multiple compression mechanisms, different font formats, and a mixture of vector and raster graphics together with a wide variety of metadata and ancillary content. We take a brief tour of these elements here, for context—they are covered more fully in later chapters.

Text and Fonts

A PDF file can contain text drawn from multiple fonts of all popular formats (Type1, TrueType, OpenType, etc). Legacy bitmap fonts are also supported through simulation. Font files are embedded in the document, so the character shapes are always available, meaning the file should render the same on any computer. A variety of character encodings are supported, including Unicode.

Text can be filled with any color, pattern, or transparency. A piece of text may be used as a shape to clip other content, allowing complicated graphical effects whilst text remains selectable and editable.

Typically, enough information is encoded in a PDF document to allow text extraction, though the process is not always straightforward.

Vector Images

Graphical content in PDF is based on the model first used in Adobe's PostScript language. It consists of *paths* built from straight lines and curves. Each path may be filled, "stroked" to draw a line, or both. Lines can have varying thicknesses, join styles, and dash patterns.

Paths may be filled in any color, with a repeating pattern defined by other objects, or with a smooth gradient between two colors. All these options apply also to the lines of stroked paths.

Paths can be rendered using a variety of plain or gradient transparencies, with several different *blend modes* defining how semitransparent objects interact. Objects may be grouped together for the purposes of transparency, so a single transparency can be applied to a whole group of objects at once.

Paths can be used to clip other objects, so that only sections of those objects overlapping with the clipping path are shown. These clipping regions may be nested within one another.

PDF has a mechanism which allows a graphic to be defined once and then used multiple times in different contexts. This can be used, for instance, for a recurring motif, even across more than one page.

Raster Images

PDF documents can include bitmap images between 1 and 16 bits per component, in several *color spaces* (for example, three-component RGB or four-component CMYK). Images can be compressed using a variety of lossless and lossy compression mechanisms.

Images may be placed at any scale or rotation, used to create a fill pattern, and may have a *mask*, which defines how they blend with the background they are placed on.

Color Spaces

PDF can use color spaces related to particular electronic or print devices (grayscale, RGB, CMYK) and ones related to human color perception. In addition, there are color spaces for the printing industry such as *spot colors*. Mechanisms exist for simpler PDF programs (like onscreen viewers) to fall back to basic color spaces if they do not support the more advanced ones.

Metadata

PDF documents have a set of standard metadata, such as *title, author, keywords,* and so on. These are defined outside the graphical content and have no effect on the document when viewed. The creator (the program that created the content) and producer (the program that wrote the PDF file) are also recorded. Each document also has a set of unique identifiers, allowing them to be tracked through a workflow.

Since PDF 1.4, the metadata can be stored in an XML (eXtensible Markup Language) document embedded in the PDF using Adobe's Extensible Metadata Platform (XMP), described in ISO 16684-1. This defines a way to store metadata for objects in the PDF, which can be extended by third parties to hold information relevant to their particular workflows or products.

Navigation

PDF documents have two methods of navigation, when viewed on screen:

- The *document outline*, commonly known as the document's *bookmarks*, is a structured list of destinations within the document, shown alongside it. Clicking on one moves the view to that page or position.
- Hyperlinks within the text or graphics of a document allow the user to click to move elsewhere within the document, or to open an external URL.

Optional Content

Optional content groups in PDF allow parts of the content of a page to be grouped together and shown—or not shown—based on some other factor (user choice, whether the document is on screen or printed, the zoom factor). Relationships between groups can be defined, so that they depend upon one another. One use for this is to emulate the "layers" found in graphics packages. For example, Adobe Illustrator layers are preserved when a document it produces is read with a PDF viewer.

Multimedia

PDF documents can include various kinds of multimedia elements. A lot of this breaks the portability inherent in PDF, and is often not well supported outside of Adobe products.

From PDF 1.1
> Slide shows can be defined, to move automatically between pages with transition effects.

From PDF 1.2
> Sounds and movies can be embedded.

From PDF 1.5
> A more general system for including arbitrary media types was introduced.

From PDF 1.6
> 3D Artwork can be embedded.

Interactive Forms

There are two incompatible forms architectures in PDF: AcroForms, which is an open standard, and the Adobe XML Forms Architecture (XFA), which is documented but requires commercial software from Adobe.

Forms allow users to fill in text fields, and use check boxes and radio buttons. When the data is complete, it may be saved into the document (if allowed) or submitted to a URL for further processing. Embedded JavaScript is often used in conjunction with forms to deal with verification of field values or similar tasks.

Logical Structure and Reflow

Logical structure facilities allow information about the structural content (chapters, sections, figures, tables, and footnotes) to be included alongside the graphical content. The particular elements are customizable by third parties.

A *tagged PDF* is one that has logical structure based on a set of Adobe-defined elements. Files following these conventions can be *reflowed* by a reader to display the same text in a different page size or text size, for example, in an ebook reader.

Security

PDF documents can be encrypted for security, using RC4 or AES encryption methods. There are two passwords—the *owner password* and the *user password*. The owner password unlocks the file for all changes, the user password just allows a range of operations selected by the owner when the file was originally encrypted (for example, allowing or disallowing printing or text extraction). Frequently the user password is blank, so the file appears to open as normal, but functionality is restricted.

Starting with PDF 1.3, digital signatures can be used to authenticate the identity of a user or the contents of the document.

Compression

Images and other data streams in PDF can be compressed using a variety of lossless and lossy methods defined by third parties. By compressing only these streams (rather than the whole file), the structure of the PDF objects is always available without decompressing the whole file, and compressed sections can be processed only when needed. There are several groups of compression methods:

- Compression for bi-level (e.g., black and white) images. PDF supports the standard lossless fax encoding methods for bi-level images and, from PDF 1.4, the JBIG2 standard (both lossy and lossless), which provides better compression for the same class of images.

- Image filters suitable for photographic data such as JPEG and, from PDF 1.5, JPEG2000 in both lossy and lossless variants.
- Lossless compression mechanisms suitable for image data and general data compression, such as Flate (the zip algorithm), Lempel-Ziv-Welch (LZW), and run length encoding.

Who Uses PDF?

PDF is used in a wide variety of industries and professions. We describe some here, explaining why PDF is suitable for each.

The Printing Industry

PDF has support for the color spaces, page dimension information (such as media, crop, art, and bleed boxes), trapping support, and resolution-independence required for commercial printing. Together with other technologies, PDF is the key part of the publishing-for-print workflow. The extensibility of PDF metadata allows various schemes for including extra data along with the document, and for keeping it with the document throughout the publishing process—parts of the workflow that don't understand a particular piece of metadata will at least preserve it.

Ebooks and Publishing

This book was created using the *DocBook* system, which takes a structured document in XML format, typesets it, and produces a PDF complete with hyperlinks and bookmarks, together with a more traditional PDF suitable for printing.

PDF is one of the competing ebook formats. To support display on a wide range of screens, PDF documents may be tagged with reflow information, allowing lines of text to be displayed at differing widths on each device. This is at odds with the other uses of PDF, where fixed text layout is a requirement.

PDF Forms

PDF forms are especially useful when existing paper-based systems are being transitioned to electronic ones, or must exist alongside them. A PDF form (filled in online then printed out) looks the same as one filled in manually on paper, and may be processed by existing human and computer systems in the same way.

Automatic submission of forms from within the PDF viewer, the use of JavaScript to add intelligence (making sure figures add up in a tax form, for example), and the use of digital signatures to sign filled-in forms are all compelling reasons to use PDF for electronic forms.

Document Archiving

Through PDF/A, PDF is the ideal format for long-term archiving, combining accurate representations of scanned and electronic content, together with Unicode language support, and compression mechanisms for all sorts of data including the important CCITT Fax and JBIG2 methods for monochrome images. Being an ISO standard (and one that is near-ubiquitous) guarantees that these documents can be read long into the future.

PDF can be used for Optical Character Recognition (OCR), allowing searchable text to be created from the original, the exact visual representation being retained alongside the recognized text.

As a File Format

PDF is not, at first sight, suitable for use as an editable vector graphics format. For example, a circle won't remain editable as a circle, since it will have been converted to a number of curves (there is no circle element in PDF).

However, if appropriate use is made of its extensibility to store auxiliary data, it makes a good solution. Adobe Illustrator, for example, now uses an extended form of PDF as its file format. The file can be viewed in any PDF viewer, but Illustrator can make use of the extended data when it is loaded back into the program.

Useful Free Software

In this book, we use various pieces of software to help us with examples. Luckily, everything you need is freely available. You'll need a PDF viewer:

- *Acrobat Reader (http://get.adobe.com/reader/)* is Adobe's own PDF viewer. It supports all versions and features of PDF and comes with a browser plug-in on most platforms. It's available for Microsoft Windows, Mac OS X, Linux, Solaris, and Android.
- *Preview* is the pre-installed PDF viewer and browser plug-in for PDF documents on Mac OS X. It's highly capable and very fast, but doesn't support everything that Acrobat Reader does. Many people stick with Preview as the default application for PDF files, but install Acrobat Reader as well.
- *Xpdf (http://foolabs.com/xpdf)* is an open source PDF viewer for Unix. It supports a reasonable subset of PDF.
- *gv (http://pages.cs.wisc.edu/~ghost/gv/index.htm)* is a PostScript and PDF viewer frontend for GhostScript (see below). It can render the textual and graphical content of almost all documents. However, it lacks most of the interactive features of other PDF viewers.

There are two key command-line tools:

- *pdftk (http://www.pdflabs.com/tools/pdftk-the-pdf-toolkit/)* is a multiplatform command-line tool for processing PDF files in various ways. It can be downloaded in pre-built form for Microsoft Windows, Mac OS X, and Linux, as well as in source code form.

- *Ghostscript (http://pages.cs.wisc.edu/~ghost/)* is a set of tools including an interpreter for PostScript and PDF. It can be used to render PDF files, and to process them in various ways from the command line. It is available in binary form for Microsoft Windows, and in source code form for all platforms.

A full discussion of Adobe and open source PDF software is in Chapter 10.

CHAPTER 2

Building a Simple PDF

In this chapter, we'll build PDF content manually in a text editor. Then we'll use the free *pdftk* program to turn it into a valid PDF file and look at the output in a PDF viewer.

This example, together with all the PDF files in this book, can be downloaded from the web page for this book (*http://oreilly.com/catalog/0636920021483*).

We'll be looking at a lot of new concepts all at once, so don't worry if it seems overwhelming—we'll come back to all of this in future chapters.

---

pdftk—The PDF Toolkit

pdftk is a free, open source command-line tool for Microsoft Windows, Mac OS X, and Unix. We're going to use it in this chapter (and throughout this book) to turn PDF content we've written in a text editor into a valid PDF file. *pdftk* can also be used to:

> Merge and split PDF documents
> Rotate PDF pages
> Decrypt and encrypt
> Fill PDF forms with data
> Apply watermarks and stamps
> Print and change PDF metadata
> Attach files to PDF documents

Source and binary packages for *pdftk* can be found at PDF Labs (*http://www.pdflabs .com/tools/pdftk-the-pdf-toolkit*).

The creator of *pdftk*, Sid Steward, is also the author of O'Reilly's *PDF Hacks*—a selection of tools and tips for working with PDF.

Basic PDF Syntax

A PDF file contains at least three distinct languages:

- The *document content*, which is a number of objects with links between them forming a *directed graph*. These objects describe the structure of the document (pages, metadata, fonts, and resources).

- The *page content*, described using a series of operators for placing text and graphics on a single page.

- The *file structure*, consisting of a *header*, *trailer*, and *cross-reference table* helping programs to locate and read the document's contents.

Document Content

The document content consists of objects built out of, amongst others, the following elements:

- Names, written as /Name.

- Integers, like 50.

- Strings, introduced with parentheses, like (The Quick Brown Fox).

- References to other objects like 2 0 R, a reference to object 2.

- Arrays (ordered collections) of objects, like [50 30 /Fred], an array of three items, in order: 50, 30, and /Fred.

- Dictionaries (unordered maps from names to objects), like << /Three 3 /Five 5 >>, which maps /Three to 3 and /Five to 5.

- Streams, which consist of a dictionary and some binary data. These are used to store streams of PDF graphics operators, and other binary data such as images and fonts.

For example, here's a *page object*, which is a dictionary containing a number of items, each associated with a name:

```
<< /Type /Page
   /MediaBox [0 0 612 792]
   /Resources 3 0 R
   /Parent 1 0 R
   /Contents [4 0 R]
>>
```

This dictionary contains five entries:

/Type /Page
> The name /Page is associated with the dictionary key /Type.

/MediaBox [0 0 612 792]
> The array of four integers [0 0 612 792] is associated with the dictionary key /MediaBox.

```
/Resources 3 0 R
```
   Object number 3 is associated with the dictionary key /Resources.

```
/Parent 1 0 R
```
   Object number 1 is associated with the dictionary key /Parent.

```
/Contents [4 0 R]
```
   The one-element array of indirect references [4 0 R] is associated with the dictionary key /Contents.

Page Content

The page content is a list of operators, each of which is preceded by zero or more operands. Here's a series of operators for selecting the /F0 font at 36 points and placing text at the current position:

```
/F0 36.0 Tf
(Hello, World!) Tj
```

Here, Tf and Tj are the operators, and /F0, 36.0, and (Hello, World!) are the operands. You can see that some syntactic elements (names and strings, for example) are shared across the languages used for both page content and document content.

File Structure

The file structure consists of:

- A *header* to distinguish the file as a PDF document.
- A *cross-reference table* listing the byte offsets of each object in the document—this allows the objects to be accessed arbitrarily, rather than having to be read in order.
- The *trailer*, which includes the byte offset of the cross-reference table, followed by an end-of-file marker.

When writing our example file, we'll use incomplete values for a lot of the file structure, relying on *pdftk* to fill in the details. For example, it's impractical for us to write the cross-reference table manually.

Document Structure

The example we'll be building is just about the simplest meaningful PDF file. However, it needs a surprisingly large number of elements. In addition to the file structure we've described above, a minimal PDF document must have a number of basic sections present:

- The *trailer dictionary*, which provides information about how to read the rest of the objects in the file.
- The *document catalog*, which is the root of the object graph.

- The *page tree*, which enumerates the pages in the document.
- At least one *page*. Each page must have:
  - — Its *resources*, which include, for example, fonts.
  - — Its *page content*, which contains the instructions for drawing text and graphics on the page.

This arrangement is illustrated in Figure 2-1.

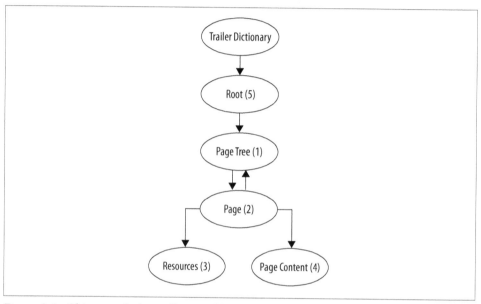

Figure 2-1. Object graph for Hello, World! PDF, with object numbers in parentheses from Example 2-1

Building the Elements

We'll type the PDF data into a text file. The line endings chosen by your text editor are unimportant (<LF> [Unix and Mac OS X] and <CR><LF> [Microsoft Windows] are both fine). We're going to skip some information (the data that is hard to work out manually), relying on *pdftk* to fill it in afterward. We will:

- Use an abbreviated header.
- Miss out the length of the page content stream, so we don't have to manually count the number of bytes.
- Omit almost all of the cross-reference table.
- Use 0 for the byte offset of the cross-reference table, again to avoid having to count it manually.

First, we'll look at the sections of the file (in the order in which they appear) and then we'll put them together and run *pdftk* to make a valid PDF file.

File Header

The file header usually consists of two lines. The first identifies the file as a PDF and gives its version number:

```
%PDF-1.1  PDF version 1.1 header
```

The second line is hard to type into a text editor since it contains nonprintable characters. We'll have *pdftk* do this for us.

Main Objects

On to the main body of the file—the objects. The first is the *page list*, which is a dictionary linking to the page objects in the document.

```
1 0 obj  Object 1
<< /Type /Pages  It's a page list
   /Count 1  There is one page
   /Kids [2 0 R]  List of object numbers of pages. Just object 2 here.
>>
endobj  End of object 1
```

Next up is the *page*. Again, it's a dictionary. It contains the paper size, an indirect reference back to the page list, and to the graphical content and *resources*.

```
2 0 obj
<< /Type /Page  It's a page
   /MediaBox [0 0 612 792]  Paper size is US Letter Portrait (612 points by 792 points)
   /Resources 3 0 R  Reference to resources at object 3
   /Parent 1 0 R  Reference back up to parent page list
   /Contents [4 0 R]  Graphical content is in object 4
>>
endobj
```

Now, the *resources*. Here, there is just one entry, the *font dictionary*, which in our example contains a single font, which we're going to use to write some text on the page.

```
3 0 obj
<< /Font  The font dictionary
     << /F0  Just one font, called /F0
         << /Type /Font  These three lines reference the built-in font Times Italic
            /BaseFont /Times-Italic
            /Subtype /Type1 >>
     >>
>>
endobj
```

Graphical Content

The *page content stream* contains a sequence of operators for placing text and graphics on the page. It was linked to by the /Contents entry in the page dictionary.

A stream object consists of a dictionary followed by a raw data stream, containing a series of PDF operands and operators. Normally, this would be compressed to reduce file size, but we're typing it in manually, so we don't compress it. We must also specify the length of the stream in bytes—*pdftk* will add the required /Length entry to the stream dictionary for us.

```
4 0 obj  The page content stream
<< >>
stream  Beginning of stream
1. 0. 0. 1. 50. 700. cm  Position at (50, 700)
BT  Begin text block
  /F0 36. Tf  Select /F0 font at 36pt
  (Hello, World!) Tj  Place the text string
ET  End text block
endstream  End of stream
endobj
```

The result of this stream of graphics operators on the page is shown in Figure 2-2.

Catalog, Cross-Reference Table, and Trailer

The last part of the file starts with the *document catalog*, which is the root object of the object graph. There follows the *cross-reference table*, which gives the byte offsets of each object in the file. We'll have *pdftk* fill this in for us. There are two final lines: one gives the byte offset of the start of the cross-reference table (we write 0 and *pdftk* will replace it for us). Finally, the end-of-file marker %%EOF.

```
5 0 obj
<< /Type /Catalog  The document catalog
   /Pages 1 0 R  Reference to the page list
>>
endobj
xref  Start of cross-reference table, which we have missed out
0 6
trailer
<< /Size 6  Number of lines in cross-reference table (number of objects plus one)
   /Root 5 0 R  Reference to the document catalog
>>
startxref
0  Byte offset of start of xref table, which we have set to 0
%%EOF  End of file marker
```

Now we're ready to put these pieces together.

Figure 2-2. The result of our graphics operators on the page

Putting it Together

The source for this file (Example 2-1) can be found in the online resources for this book (*http://oreilly.com/catalog/0636920021483*), or you can type it in yourself. Save it as *hello-broken.pdf*.

Example 2-1. The invalid hello-broken.pdf PDF file suitable for manual creation

```
%PDF-1.1 File header
1 0 obj Main objects
<< /Type /Pages
   /Count 1
   /Kids [2 0 R]
>>
endobj
2 0 obj
<< /Type /Page
   /MediaBox [0 0 612 792]
   /Resources 3 0 R
   /Parent 1 0 R
   /Contents [4 0 R]
>>
endobj
3 0 obj
<< /Font
    << /F0
       << /Type /Font
          /BaseFont /Times-Italic
          /Subtype /Type1 >>
    >>
>>
endobj
4 0 obj Graphical content
<< >>
stream
1. 0. 0. 1. 50. 700. cm
BT
  /F0 36. Tf
  (Hello, World!) Tj
ET
endstream
endobj
5 0 obj Catalog, cross-reference table, and trailer
<< /Type /Catalog
   /Pages 1 0 R
>>
endobj
xref
0 6
trailer
<< /Size 6
   /Root 5 0 R
>>
```

```
startxref
0
%%EOF
```

As it stands, `hello-broken.pdf` is not a valid PDF file, and even Adobe Reader (which is fairly tolerant of malformed files) won't cope with it.

We can use the free *pdftk* tool to fix up the *hello-broken.pdf* file with the missing details, writing the output to *hello.pdf*:

`pdftk hello-broken.pdf output hello.pdf`

pdftk reads the file and its objects, and calculates the correct data for the missing or incorrect sections we wrote, and produces the valid file shown in Example 2-2. Note that the spacing and formatting of some of the syntax has been altered—each PDF producer makes slightly different choices about this.

Example 2-2. The completed PDF file hello.pdf, fixed by pdftk

```
%PDF-1.1
%âãÏÓ ❶
1 0 obj
<<
/Kids [2 0 R]
/Count 1
/Type /Pages
>>
endobj
2 0 obj
<<
/Rotate 0
/Parent 1 0 R
/Resources 3 0 R
/MediaBox [0 0 612 792]
/Contents [4 0 R]
/Type /Page
>>
endobj
3 0 obj
<<
/Font
<<
/F0
<<
/BaseFont /Times-Italic
/Subtype /Type1
/Type /Font
>>
>>
>>
endobj
4 0 obj
<<
/Length 65 ❷
>>
```

```
stream
1. 0. 0. 1. 50. 700. cm
BT
  /F0 36. Tf
  (Hello, World!) Tj
ET

endstream
endobj
5 0 obj
<<
/Pages 1 0 R
/Type /Catalog
>>
endobj xref
0 6 ❸
0000000000 65535 f
0000000015 00000 n
0000000074 00000 n
0000000192 00000 n
0000000291 00000 n
0000000409 00000 n
trailer

<<
/Root 5 0 R
/Size 6
>>
startxref
459 ❹
%%EOF
```

❶ Some nonprintable characters have been added to the PDF header—this ensures that the file is recognized as binary (rather than text) by, for example, file transfer programs such as FTP.

❷ The length in bytes of the stream has been filled in.

❸ The cross-reference table has been filled in with the byte offsets of each object in the file.

❹ The byte offset of the start of the cross-reference table has been filled in.

The file can now be loaded into a PDF viewer. The result in Acrobat Reader on Microsoft Windows is shown in Figure 2-3.

Figure 2-3. Hello, World! PDF, viewed in the free Adobe Reader on Microsoft Windows

Remarks

We've seen how to build a simple PDF file from scratch, using *pdftk* to help us, and we've looked at some of the basic syntax that makes up a PDF document.

You can look at existing PDF files using your text editor too. However, some of the data (such as the graphics operators making up the page content) is likely to be compressed and thus unreadable. The *pdftk* command can be used to decompress these sections for easier reading—see "Compression" on page 114.

In future chapters, we'll look at the parts of a typical PDF file in some detail and how programs read, write, and edit PDF files. At each stage, there will be the opportunity to build example files by altering and extending the example we built in this chapter.

CHAPTER 3

File Structure

In this chapter, we describe the layout and content of the PDF file's four main sections, and the syntax of the objects which make up each one. We also outline the process of reading a PDF file into a high level data structure, and the converse operation of writing that structure to a PDF file.

File Layout

A simple valid PDF file has four parts, in order:

1. The *header*, which gives the PDF version number.

2. The *body*, containing the pages, graphical content, and much of the ancillary information, all encoded as a series of *objects*.

3. The *cross-reference table*, which lists the position of each object within the file, to facilitate random access.

4. The *trailer* including the *trailer dictionary*, which helps to locate each part of the file and lists various pieces of metadata which can be read without processing the whole file.

For reference, we reproduce the "Hello, World" PDF from Chapter 2 as Example 3-1. The first line of each of the four sections has been annotated.

Example 3-1. A small PDF file

```
%PDF-1.1 Header starts here
%âãÏÓ
1 0 obj Body starts here
<<
/Kids [2 0 R]
/Count 1
/Type /Pages
>>
endobj
2 0 obj
<<
```

```
/Rotate 0
/Parent 1 0 R
/Resources 3 0 R
/MediaBox [0 0 612 792]
/Contents [4 0 R]
/Type /Page
>>
endobj
3 0 obj
<<
/Font
<<
/F0
<<
/BaseFont /Times-Italic
/Subtype /Type1
/Type /Font
>>
>>
>>
endobj
4 0 obj
<<
/Length 65
>>
stream
1. 0. 0. 1. 50. 700. cm
BT
  /F0 36. Tf
  (Hello, World!) Tj
ET
endstream
endobj
5 0 obj
<<
/Pages 1 0 R
/Type /Catalog
>>
endobj
xref    Cross-reference table starts here
0 6
0000000000 65535 f
0000000015 00000 n
0000000074 00000 n
0000000192 00000 n
0000000291 00000 n
0000000409 00000 n
trailer   Trailer starts here
<<
/Root 5 0 R
/Size 6
>>
startxref
459
%%EOF
```

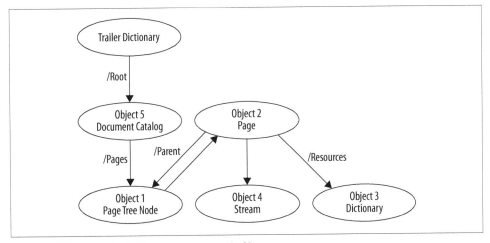

Figure 3-1. The graph of objects in our example file

We now take a closer look at each of these four parts in turn, using Example 3-1 for reference.

Header

The first line of a PDF file gives the version number of the document. In our example, this is:

```
%PDF-1.1
```

This defines the file as PDF version 1.1 (PDF version 1.0 was a 7-bit ASCII format, rather than an 8-bit binary format, so nowadays we only create files PDF version 1.1 or later). PDF is backward compatible, so a PDF 1.3 document should be readable by a program which knows about, for example, PDF 1.5. It is also, for the most part, forward compatible, so most PDF programs will attempt to read any file, no matter what the supposed version number is.

Since PDF files almost always contain binary data, they can become corrupted if line endings are changed (for example, if the file is transferred over FTP in text mode). To allow legacy file transfer programs to determine that the file is binary, it is usual to include some bytes with character codes higher than 127 in the header. For example:

```
%âãïó
```

The percent sign indicates a comment, the other few bytes are arbitrary character codes in excess of 127. So, the whole header in our example is:

```
%PDF-1.1
%âãïó
```

Body

The file body consists of a sequence of objects, each preceded by an *object number*, *generation number*, and the obj keyword on one line, and followed by the endobj keyword on another. For example:

```
1 0 obj
<<
/Kids [2 0 R]
/Count 1
/Type /Pages
>>
endobj
```

Here, the object number is 1, and the generation number is 0 (it almost always is). The content for object 1 is in between the two lines 1 0 obj and endobj. In this case, it's the dictionary <</Kids [2 0 R] /Count 1 /Type /Pages>>.

Cross-Reference Table

The cross-reference table lists the byte offset of each object in the file body. This allows random access to the objects, so that they do not have to be read in order, and an object which is never used is never read. This means, in particular, that simple operations like counting the number of pages in a PDF document can be fast, even on large files.

Every object in a PDF file has an *object number* and a *generation number*. Generation numbers are used when a cross reference table entry is reused—we don't consider them here (they will always be zero).

For our purposes, we can consider the cross-reference table to consist of a header line indicating the number of entries, then a special entry, then one line for each object in the file body. In our file:

```
0 6         Six entries in table, starting at 0
0000000000 65535 f  Special entry
0000000015 00000 n  Object 1 is at byte offset 15
0000000074 00000 n  Object 2 is at byte offset 74
0000000192 00000 n  etc...
```

```
0000000291 00000 n
0000000409 00000 n  Object 5 is at byte offset 409
```

Note that the byte offsets are stored with leading zeros to ensure each entry is the same length. Thus, we can read the cross-reference table with random access too.

Trailer

The first line of the trailer is just the `trailer` keyword. This is followed by the *trailer dictionary*, which contains at least the `/Size` entry (which gives the number of entries in the cross-reference table) and the `/Root` entry (which gives the object number of the *document catalog*, which is the root element of the graph of objects in the body).

There follows a line with just the `startxref` keyword, a line with a single number (the byte offset of the start of the cross-reference table within the file), and then the line %%EOF, which signals the end of the PDF file.

Here's the trailer from Example 3-1:

```
trailer   Trailer keyword
<<   The trailer dictinonary
/Root 5 0 R
/Size 6
>>
startxref   startxref keyword
459   Byte offset of cross-reference table
%%EOF   End-of-file marker
```

The trailer is read from the end of the file backwards: the end-of-file marker is found, the byte offset of the cross-reference table extracted, and then the trailer dictionary parsed. The `trailer` keyword marks the upper extent of the trailer.

Lexical Conventions

A PDF file is a sequence of 8 bit bytes. Using the rules we describe in this chapter, these characters can be grouped into *tokens* (such as keywords and numbers), and the file parsed.

Some general rules apply to the main body of the file, and frequently to the various other languages in a PDF file. There are three kinds of characters: *regular characters*, *whitespace characters*, and *delimiters*. The whitespace characters are listed in Table 3-1. The delimiters are ( ) < > [ ] { } / %, and are used to define arrays, dictionaries and so on. All other characters are regular characters, with no special meaning.

Table 3-1. Whitespace characters

Character code	Meaning
0	Null
9	Tab
10	Line feed
12	Form feed
13	Carriage return
32	Space

PDF files can use <CR>, <LF>, or a <CR><LF> sequence to end a line. Note, however, that changing the line endings en masse (for example, in a text editor) will likely corrupt the file, since it will alter any line ending sequences that happen to occur in the midst of compressed binary data sections, and may alter the length of objects, invalidating the cross-reference table.

Objects

PDF supports five basic objects:

- Integers and real numbers, such as 42 and 3.1415.
- Strings, which are enclosed in parentheses. For example (The Quick Brown Fox).
- Names, which are used for keys in dictionaries, and innumerable other purposes. They are introduced with a /, for example /Blue.
- Boolean values, denoted by the keywords true and false.
- The null object, denoted by the keyword null.

and three compound objects:

- Arrays, which contain an ordered collection of other objects such as [1 0 0].
- Dictionaries, which consist of an unordered collection of pairs, mapping names to objects. For example, <</Contents 4 0 R /Resources 5 0 R>>, which maps /Contents to the indirect reference 4 0 R and /Resources to the indirect reference 5 0 R.
- Streams, which hold binary data, together with a dictionary describing attributes of the data such as its length and any compression parameters. Streams are used to store images, fonts and so on.

and a way of linking objects together:

- The indirect reference, which forms a link from one object to another.

A PDF file consists of a graph of objects, with indirect references forming the links between them. The object graph for Example 3-1 is shown in Figure 3-1.

Integers and Real Numbers

An integer is written as one or more of the decimal digits `0..9` optionally preceded by a plus or minus sign:

```
0    +1    -1    63
```

A real number is written as one or more decimal digits optionally preceded by a plus or minus sign, and optionally having one decimal point, which may be leading, inside, or following:

```
0.0    0.    .0    -0.004    65.4
```

Frequently, the specification allows a given object to be either an integer or a real number. Other times it must be an integer. In addition, the range and accuracy of integers and reals is defined by the PDF implementation, not the standard. In certain implementations, if an integer exceeds the range available, it is converted to a real number.

 Exponential notation is not allowed. For example, you can't write `4.5e-6`.

Strings

Strings consist of a series of bytes, written between parentheses:

```
(Hello, World!)
```

The backslash \ character and the parenthesis characters ( ) must be escaped by preceding them with a backslash. For example, writing:

```
(Some \\ escaped \(characters)
```

represents the string "`Some \ escaped (characters`". Balanced pairs of parentheses within the string need not be escaped. For example, `(Red (Rouge))` represents the string "`Red (Rouge)`".

A backslash can also be used to introduce other character codes for readability purposes (see Table 3-2).

Table 3-2. Escape sequences in strings

Character sequence	Meaning
\n	Line feed
\r	Carriage return
\t	Horizontal tab
\b	Backspace
\f	Form feed
\ *ddd*	Character code in three octal digits

After the string is read from the file, and the escaped characters resolved to yield the series of bytes forming the string proper, it may then be interpreted as described in "Text Strings" on page 45.

Hexadecimal strings

Strings can also be written as a sequence of hexadecimal digits between < and >, each pair representing a byte:

    `<4F6Eff00>` *Bytes 0x4F, 0x6E, 0xFF, and 0x00*

When there is an odd number of digits, the last is assumed to be 0. Hexadecimal strings are typically used to make binary data user-readable. It is functionally the same as describing strings in the usual way.

Names

Names are used throughout PDF, as keys for dictionaries and to define various multi-valued objects where using integers to enumerate them would be unintuitive. A name is introduced with the forward slash. For example:

    `/French`

The / character is part of the name—in fact, / on its own is a valid name. The name may not contain whitespace or delimiters, but where a name needs to correspond to some external name which has these characters (for example, spaces), we can use a hash sign followed by two decimal digits:

    `/Websafe#20Dark#20Green`

This represents the name `/Websafe Dark Green` since, in ASCII, hexadecimal 20 is the code for space. Names are case-sensitive (`/French` and `/french` are different).

Boolean Values

PDF allows the Boolean values `true` and `false`. They are frequently used as flags in dictionary entries.

Arrays

An array represents an ordered collection of PDF objects, including other arrays. The objects need not all be of the same type. For example, the array:

    `[0 0 400 500]`

contains four numbers in order: 0, 0, 400, 500. The array:

    `[/Green /Blue [/Red /Yellow]]`

contains three items: the name `/Green`, the name `/Blue` and the array of two names `[/Red /Yellow]`.

Dictionaries

A dictionary represents an unordered collection of *key-value pairs*. The dictionary maps the keys to the values—provide a key, and the value is the result of looking it up in the dictionary. The keys are names, the values may be any PDF object. Dictionaries are written between << and >>. For example:

```
<</One 1 /Two 2 /Three 3>>
```

maps the name /One to the integer 1, the name /Two to the integer 2, and the name /Three to the integer 3. Dictionaries can, of course, contain other dictionaries. Nested dictionaries form the bulk of the non-graphical structured data in most PDF files.

Indirect References

In order to split the PDF content over separate objects (so data may be read only if required), we connect them together with *indirect references*. The indirect reference to object 6 is written as:

```
6 0 R
```

Here, 6 is the object number, 0 is the generation number (which we don't consider here), and R is the indirect reference keyword.

For example, here's a typical dictionary using indirect references:

```
<< /Resources 10 0 R
   /Contents [4 0 R] >>
```

In this example, objects 10 and 4 are being referenced in the values of a dictionary.

Streams and Filters

Streams are used to store binary data. They are formed of a dictionary followed by a chunk of binary data. The dictionary lists the length of the data, and optionally other parameters, according to the particular use to which the stream is put.

Syntactically, a stream consists of a dictionary, followed by the stream keyword, a new-line (<LF> or <CR><LF>), zero or more bytes of data, another newline, and finally the endstream keyword. From our example file:

```
4 0 obj  Object 4
<<
/Length 65  Length of the data
>>
stream  Stream keyword
1. 0. 0. 1. 50. 700. cm  65 bytes of data, here a graphics stream
BT
  /F0 36. Tf
  (Hello, World!) Tj
```

```
ET
endstream  endstream keyword
endobj  end of object
```

Here, the dictionary just contains the /Length entry, which gives the length of the stream in bytes.

All streams must be indirect objects. Streams are almost always compressed, using a variety of mechanisms, which are listed in Table 3-3.

Table 3-3. PDF stream compression methods

Method name	Description
/ASCIIHexDecode	Produces one byte of uncompressed data for each pair of hexadecimal digits in the compressed data. > indicates end of data. Whitespace is ignored. This filter and /ASCII85Decode are intended to reduce data to 7 bits—/ASCII85Decode is more complicated, but more compact.
/ASCII85Decode	This 7-bit encoding uses the printable characters ! through u and z. The sequence ~> indicates end of data.
/LZWDecode	Implements Lempel-Ziv-Welch compression, as used by the TIFF image format.
/FlateDecode	Flate compression, as used by the open source zlib library. Defined in RFC 1950. Both /LZWDecode and /FlateDecode can have *predictors* in the stream dictionary, which define postprocessing on the data to reverse pre-processing which was done when it was compressed.
/RunLengthDecode	A simple byte-based run-length compressor.
/CCITTFaxDecode	Implements Group 3 and Group 4 encoding, as used by fax machines. Works well on monochrome (1bpp) images, not for general data.
/JBIG2Decode	A more modern, better compression mechanism for the kinds of data suitable for use with /CCITTFaxDecode. Implements the JBIG2 compression method.
/DCTDecode	JPEG lossy compression. Whole JPEG files can be put in here, complete with all the headers.
/JPXDecode	JPEG2000 lossy and lossless compression. Limited to the JPX baseline set of features, with a few exceptions.

Here's an example of a compressed stream:

```
796 0 obj
<</Length 275 /Filter /FlateDecode>>
stream
HTKOo÷ü  And 268 more bytes...
endstream
endobj
```

Multiple filters can be used, by specifying an array instead of a name for the /Filter entry in the stream's dictionary.

For example, an image compressed with the JPEG method then ASCII85 encoded, might have the following filter entry:

```
/Filter [/ASCII85Decode /DCTDecode]
```

Filters which require external parameters (for example, defining compression parameters outside the data stream itself) store those in the stream dictionary too.

Incremental Update

Incremental update allows a file to be updated by appending modifications to the end of the file, so the whole file doesn't need to be written again (which, for a large file, could take a long time). The update constitutes the new or changed objects, and an update to the cross-reference table. This means saving the changes takes less time, but the file may become bloated (because objects which are no longer needed cannot be deleted).

This updating process may happen several times. A side-effect is that files updated in this fashion may have those changes undone one or more levels, to retrieve earlier versions of the document.

When altering a digitally signed document, all updates must be made incrementally—otherwise, the digital signature would be invalidated. The recipient can undo the incremental updates to retrieve the original, certified document.

When a file is updated incrementally, a new trailer is added, containing all the entries from the previous trailer, together with a /Prev entry giving the byte offset of the previous cross-reference table. Thus, a file which has been incrementally updated will have multiple trailer dictionaries and end-of-file markers. In this way, a PDF application can read the cross-reference sections in reverse order to build up a list of the latest versions of each object in the file. Objects which have been replaced keep the same object number.

Object and Cross-Reference Streams

Starting with PDF 1.5, a new mechanism was introduced to further compress PDF files by allowing many objects to be put into a single *object stream*, the whole stream being compressed. In tandem, a new mechanism for referencing the objects in these streams was introduced—*cross-reference streams*.

A file will generally use several sets of object streams, grouping together objects which are needed at certain times, for example all the objects on page one, all the objects on page two, and so on. This retains the random access property of the document, which would be lost if all the objects in a file were to be put into a single object stream. Object streams can't contain other streams.

Files compressed with these mechanisms are rather hard to read manually, so we can use the `decompress` operation in *pdftk* as usual, to rewrite them decompressed for inspection. This has the side effect of writing them without object and cross-reference streams. See Chapter 9 for details.

Linearized PDF

When viewing a large PDF file in a network environment, especially when the data rate is low or the network latency high, the user does not want to wait for the whole file to download to view it. This is especially important when the document is being viewed inside a web browser.

We should like the first page to appear quickly, and for changing to another page (by clicking on a hyperlink or a bookmark) to be as fast as possible. In the case of individual pages being large (rather than just the whole document), we should like page content to appear incrementally, most-important content first. Network transport mechanisms such as HTTP (The HyperText Transfer Protocol, used for fetching web pages in a web browser) often allow an arbitrary chunk of data to be fetched. However, because of latency, we wish to fetch a single chunk with all the data for a page, rather than hundreds of little chunks, one for each object.

PDF 1.2 introduced such a mechanism, *linearized PDF*. This adds rules for how to order objects in a file and *hint tables* to indicate how such objects have been ordered. The system is backward compatible, so that a linearized PDF file is also a normal one, and may be read as such by a reader which does not understand linearized PDF.

A linearized PDF file can be recognized by the presence of a *linearization dictionary* at the top of the file, directly after the header. For example:

```
%PDF-1.4
%âãÏÓ
4 0 obj
<< /E 200967
   /H [ 667 140 ]
   /L 201431
   /Linearized 1
   /N 1
   /O 7
   /T 201230
>>
endobj
```

The *pdfopt* command-line program shipped with GhostScript can linearize a file. For example:

```
pdfopt input.pdf output.pdf
```

This linearizes `input.pdf` and writes the result to `output.pdf`.

How a PDF File is Read

To read a PDF file, converting it from a flat series of bytes into a graph of objects in memory, the following steps might typically occur:

1. Read the PDF header from the beginning of the file, checking that this is, indeed, a PDF document and retrieving its version number.

2. The end-of-file marker is now found, by searching backward from the end of the file. The trailer dictionary can now be read, and the byte offset of the start of the cross-reference table retrieved.

3. The cross-reference table can now be read. We now know where each object in the file is.

4. At this stage, all the objects can be read and parsed, or we can leave this process until each object is actually needed, reading it on demand.

5. We can now use the data, extracting the pages, parsing graphical content, extracting metadata, and so on.

This is not an exhaustive description, since there are many possible complications (encryption, linearization, objects, and cross-reference streams).

The following recursive data structure, given in psuedocode, can hold a PDF object.

```
pdfobject ::= Null
            | Boolean of bool
            | Integer of int
            | Real of real
            | String of string
            | Name of string
            | Array of pdfobject array
            | Dictionary of (string, pdfobject) array   Array of (string, pdfobject) pairs
            | Stream of (pdfobject, bytes)   Stream dictionary and stream data
            | Indirect of int
```

For example, the object `<< /Kids [2 0 R] /Count 1 /Type /Pages >>` might be represented as:

```
Dictionary
  ((Name (/Kids), Array (Indirect 2)),
   (Name (/Count), Integer (1)),
   (Name (/Type), Name (/Pages)))
```

Figure 3-1, shown earlier in the chapter, shows the object graph for the file in Example 3-1.

How a PDF File is Written

Writing a PDF document to a series of bytes in a file is much simpler than reading it—we don't need to support all of the PDF format, just the subset we intend to use. Writing a PDF file is very fast, since it amounts to little more than flattening the object graph to a series of bytes.

1. Output the header.
2. Remove any objects which are not referenced by any other object in the PDF. This avoids writing objects which are no longer needed.
3. Renumber the objects so they run from 1 to n where n is the number of objects in the file.
4. Output the objects one by one, starting with object number one, recording the byte offset of each for the cross-reference table.
5. Write the cross-reference table.
6. Write the trailer, trailer dictionary, and end-of-file marker.

CHAPTER 4

Document Structure

In this chapter, we leave behind the bits and bytes of the PDF file, and consider the logical structure. We consider the *trailer dictionary*, *document catalog*, and *page tree*. We enumerate the required entries in each object. We then look at two common structures in PDF files: *text strings* and *dates*.

Figure 4-1 shows the logical structure of a typical document.

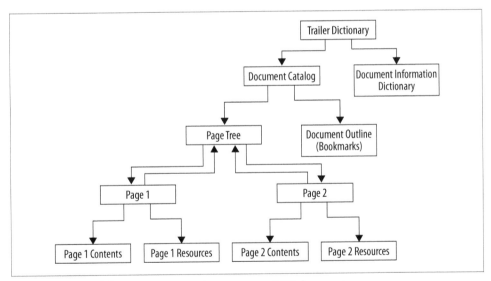

Figure 4-1. Typical document structure for a two page PDF document

Trailer Dictionary

This dictionary, residing in the file's trailer rather than the main body of the file, is one of the first things to be processed when a program wants to read a PDF document. It contains entries allowing the cross-reference table—and thus the file's objects—to be read. Its important entries are summarized in Table 4-1.

Table 4-1. Entries in a trailer dictionary (*denotes required entry)

Key	Value type	Value
/Size*	Integer	Total number of entries in the file's cross-reference table (usually equal to the number of objects in the file plus one).
/Root*	Indirect reference to dictionary	The *document catalog*.
/Info	Indirect reference to dictionary	The document's *document information dictionary*.
/ID	Array of two Strings	Uniquely identifies the file within a work flow. The first string is decided when the file is first created, the second modified by workflow systems when they modify the file.

Here's an example trailer dictionary:

```
<<
    /Size 421
    /Root 377 0 R
    /Info 375 0 R
    /ID [<75ff22189ceac848dfa2afec93deee03> <057928614d9711db835e000d937095a2>]
>>
```

Once the trailer dictionary has been processed, we can go on to read the *document information dictionary* and the *document catalog*.

Document Information Dictionary

The *document information dictionary* contains the creation and modification dates of the file, together with some simple metadata (not to be confused with the more comprehensive XMP metadata discussed in "XML Metadata" on page 93).

Document information dictionary entries are described in Table 4-2. A typical document information dictionary is given in Example 4-1.

Table 4-2. Entries in a document information dictionary. The types "text string" and "date string" are explained later in this chapter.

Key	Value type	Value
/Title	text string	The document's title. Note that this is nothing to do with any title displayed on the first page.
/Subject	text string	The subject of the document. Again, this is just metadata with no particular rules about content.
/Keywords	text string	Keywords associated with this document. No advice is given as to how to structure these.
/Author	text string	The name of the author of the document.
/CreationDate	date string	The date the document was created.

Key	Value type	Value
/ModDate	date string	The date the document was last modified.
/Creator	text string	The name of the program which originally created this document, if it started as another format (for example, "Microsoft Word").
/Producer	text string	The name of the program which converted this file to PDF, if it started as another format (for example, the format of a word processor).

Example 4-1. Typical document information dictionary

```
<<
    /ModDate (D:20060926213913+02'00')
    /CreationDate (D:20060926213913+02'00')
    /Title (catalogueproduit-UK.qxd)
    /Creator (QuarkXPress: pictwpstops filter 1.0)
    /Producer (Acrobat Distiller 6.0 for Macintosh)
    /Author (James Smith)
>>
```

The *date string* format (for /CreationDate and /ModDate) is discussed in the section "Dates" on page 45. The *text string* format (which describes how different encodings can be used within the string type) is described in "Text Strings" on page 45.

Document Catalog

The *document catalog* is the root object of the main object graph, from which all other objects may be reached through indirect references. In Table 4-3, we list the document catalog dictionary entries which are required, and some of the many optional ones, so as to introduce brief PDF topics we don't cover elsewhere in these pages.

Table 4-3. The document catalog (*denotes required entry)

Key	Value type	Value
/Type*	name	Must be /Catalog.
/Pages*	indirect reference to dictionary	The root node of the page tree. Page trees are discussed in "Pages and Page Trees" on page 42.
/PageLabels	number tree	A number tree giving the page labels for this document. This mechanism allows for pages in a document to have more complicated numbering than just 1,2,3....For example, the preface of a book may be numbered i,ii,iii..., whilst the main content starts again at 1,2,3....These page labels are displayed in PDF viewers—they have nothing to do with printed output.
/Names	dictionary	The name dictionary. This contains various *name trees*, which map names to entities, to prevent having to use object numbers to reference them directly.

Key	Value type	Value
/Dests	dictionary	A dictionary mapping names to destinations. A destination is a description of a place within a PDF document to which a hyper-link sends the user.
/ViewerPreferences	dictionary	A *viewer preferences dictionary*, which allows flags to specify the behavior of a PDF viewer when the document is viewed on screen, such as the page it is opened on, the initial viewing scale and so on.
/PageLayout	name	Specifies the page layout to be used by PDF viewers. Values are /SinglePage, /OneColumn, /TwoColumnLeft, /TwoColumnRight, /TwoPageLeft, /TwoPageRight. (Default: /SinglePage). Details are in Table 28 of ISO 32000-1:2008.
/PageMode	name	Specifies the page mode to be used by PDF viewers. Values are /UseNone, /UseOutlines, /UseThumbs, /FullScreen, /UseOC, /UseAttachments. (Default: /UseNone). Details are in Table 28 of ISO 32000-1:2008.
/Outlines	indirect reference to dictionary	The outline dictionary is the root of the *document outline*, commonly known as the bookmarks.
/Metadata	indirect reference to stream	The document's XMP metadata—see "XML Meta-data" on page 93.

Pages and Page Trees

A *page tree*, built from *page dictionaries*, brings together instructions for drawing the graphical and textual content (which we consider in Chapter 5 and Chapter 6) with the resources (fonts, images, and other external data) which those instructions make use of. It also includes the page size, together with a number of other *boxes* defining cropping and so forth.

The entries in a page dictionary are summarized in Table 4-4.

Table 4-4. Entries in a page dictionary (*denotes required entry)

Key	Value type	Value
/Type*	name	Must be /Page.
/Parent*	indirect reference to dictionary	The parent node of this node in the page tree.
/Resources	dictionary	The page's resources (fonts, images, and so on). If this entry is omitted entirely, the resources are inherited from the parent node in the page tree. If there are really no resources, include this entry but use an empty dictionary.
/Contents	indirect reference to stream or array of such references	The graphical content of the page in one or more sections. If this entry is missing, the page is empty.

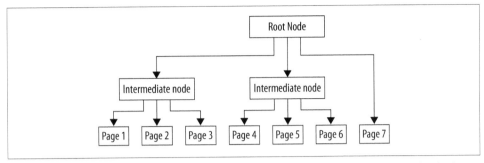

Figure 4-2. A page tree for seven pages. The exact shape of the tree is left to the individual PDF application. The PDF code for this tree is shown in Example 4-2.

Key	Value type	Value
/Rotate	integer	The viewing rotation of the page in degrees, clockwise from north. Value must be a multiple of 90. Default value: 0. This applies to both viewing and printing. If this entry is missing, its value is inherited from its parent node in the page tree.
/MediaBox*	rectangle	The page's *media box* (the size of its media, i.e., paper). For most purposes, the page size. If this entry is missing, it is inherited from its parent node in the page tree.
/CropBox	rectangle	The page's crop box. This defines the region of the page visible by default when a page is displayed or printed. If absent, its value is defined to be the same as the media box.

The *rectangle* data structure for the *media box* and the other boxes is an array of four numbers. These define the diagonally opposite corners of the rectangle—the first two elements of the array being the *x* and *y* coordinates of one corner, the latter two elements being those of the other. Normally, the lower-left and upper-right corners are given. So, for example:

```
/MediaBox [0 0 500 800]
/CropBox [100 100 400 700]
```

defines a 500 by 800 point page with a crop box removing 100 points on each side of the page.

The pages are linked together using a *page tree*, rather than a simple array. This tree structure makes it faster to find a given page in a document with hundreds or thousands of pages. Good PDF applications build a *balanced tree* (one with the minimum height for the number of nodes). This ensures that a particular page can be located quickly. The nodes with no children are the pages themselves. An example page tree structure for seven pages is shown in Figure 4-2.

This would be written in PDF objects as shown in Example 4-2. The entries in an intermediate or root page tree node (i.e., not a page itself) are summarized in Table 4-5.

Example 4-2. PDF objects used to build the page tree illustrated in Figure 4-2

```
1 0 obj  Root node
<< /Type /Pages /Kids [2 0 R 3 0 R 4 0 R] /Count 7 >>
endobj
2 0 obj  Intermediate node
<< /Type /Pages /Kids [5 0 R 6 0 R 7 0 R] /Parent 1 0 R /Count 3 >>
endobj
3 0 obj  Intermediate node
<< /Type /Pages /Kids [8 0 R 9 0 R 10 0 R] /Parent 1 0 R /Count 3 >>
endobj
4 0 obj  Page 7
<< /Type /Page /Parent 1 0 R /MediaBox [0 0 500 500] /Resources << >> >>
endobj
5 0 obj  Page 1
<< /Type /Page /Parent 2 0 R /MediaBox [0 0 500 500] /Resources << >> >>
endobj
6 0 obj  Page 2
<< /Type /Page /Parent 2 0 R /MediaBox [0 0 500 500] /Resources << >> >>
endobj
7 0 obj  Page 3
<< /Type /Page /Parent 2 0 R /MediaBox [0 0 500 500] /Resources << >> >>
endobj
8 0 obj  Page 4
<< /Type /Page /Parent 3 0 R /MediaBox [0 0 500 500] /Resources << >> >>
endobj
9 0 obj  Page 5
<< /Type /Page /Parent 3 0 R /MediaBox [0 0 500 500] /Resources << >> >>
endobj
10 0 obj  Page 6
<< /Type /Page /Parent 3 0 R /MediaBox [0 0 500 500] /Resources << >> >>
endobj
```

*Table 4-5. Entries in an intermediate or root page tree node (*denotes a required entry)*

Key	Value type	Value
/Type*	name	Must be /Pages.
/Kids*	array of indirect references	The immediate child page-tree nodes of this node.
/Count*	integer	The number of page nodes (not other page tree nodes) which are eventual children of this node.
/Parent	indirect reference to page tree node	Reference to the parent of this node (the node of which this is a child). Must be present if not the root node of the page tree.

In this tree, any page can be found at most two indirect references away from the root node.

Text Strings

Strings outside of the actual textual content of a page (e.g., bookmark names, document information etc.) are known as *text strings*. They are encoded using either *PDFDocEncoding* or (in more recent documents) Unicode. PDFDocEncoding is a based on the ISO Latin-1 Encoding. It is documented fully in Annex D of ISO Standard 32000-1:2008.

Text strings which are encoded as Unicode are distinguished by looking at the first two bytes: these will be 254 followed by 255. This is the Unicode byte-order marker U+FEFF, which indicates the UTF16BE encoding. This means a PDFDocEncoding string can't begin with þ (254) followed by ÿ (255), but this is unlikely to occur in any reasonable circumstance.

Dates

The creation and modification dates `/CreationDate` and `/ModDate` in the document information dictionary are examples of the PDF date format, which encodes a date in a string, including information about the time zone.

A date string has the format:

    (D:YYYYMMDDHHmmSSOHH'mm')

where the parentheses indicate a string as usual. The other parts of the date are summarized in Table 4-6.

Table 4-6. PDF date format constituents

Portion	Meaning
YYYY	The year, in four digits, e.g., 2008.
MM	The month, in two digits from 01 to 12.
DD	The day, in two digits from 01 to 31.
HH	The hour, in two digits from 00 to 23.
mm	The minute, in two digits from 00 to 59.
SS	The second, in two digits from 00 to 59.
O	The relationship of local time to Universal Time, either +, - or Z. + signifies local time is later than UT, - earlier, and Z equal to Universal Time.
HH'	The absolute value of the offset from Universal Time in hours, in two digits from 00 to 23.
mm'	The absolute value of the offset from Universal Time in minutes, in two digits from 00 to 59.

All parts of the date after the year are optional. For example, (D:1999) is perfectly valid. Plainly, though, if you omit one part, you must omit everything which follows, otherwise the result would be ambiguous. The default values for DD and MM is 01, for all other parts, the default is zeros.

For example:

```
(D:20060926213913+02'00')
```

represents September 26th 2006 at 9:39:13 p.m, in a time zone two hours ahead of Universal Time.

Putting it Together

This is a manually-created text, to be processed into a valid PDF file by *pdftk* using the method introduced in Chapter 2. It is a three page document, with document information dictionary and page tree. Figure 4-3 shows this document displayed in Acrobat Reader. Figure 4-4 is the corresponding object graph.

Example 4-3. A three page document with document information dictionary

```
%PDF-1.1 Header
1 0 obj Top-level of page tree: has two children—page one and an intermediate page tree node
<< /Kids [2 0 R 3 0 R] /Type /Pages /Count 3 >>
endobj
4 0 obj Contents stream for page one
<< >>
stream
1. 0.000000 0.000000 1. 50. 770. cm BT /F0 36. Tf (Page One) Tj ET
endstream
endobj
2 0 obj Page one
<<
  /Rotate 0
  /Parent 1 0 R
  /Resources
    << /Font << /F0 << /BaseFont /Times-Italic /Subtype /Type1 /Type /Font >> >> >>
  /MediaBox [0.000000 0.000000 595.275590551 841.88976378]
  /Type /Page
  /Contents [4 0 R]
>>
endobj
5 0 obj Document catalog
<< /PageLayout /TwoColumnLeft /Pages 1 0 R /Type /Catalog >>
endobj
6 0 obj Page three
<<
  /Rotate 0
  /Parent 3 0 R
  /Resources
    << /Font << /F0 << /BaseFont /Times-Italic /Subtype /Type1 /Type /Font >> >> >>
  /MediaBox [0.000000 0.000000 595.275590551 841.88976378]
  /Type /Page
```

```
    /Contents [7 0 R]
>>
endobj
3 0 obj Intermediate page tree node, linking to pages two and three
<< /Parent 1 0 R /Kids [8 0 R 6 0 R] /Count 2 /Type /Pages >>
endobj
8 0 obj Page two
<<
  /Rotate 270
  /Parent 3 0 R
  /Resources
    << /Font << /F0 << /BaseFont /Times-Italic /Subtype /Type1 /Type /Font >> >> >>
  /MediaBox [0.000000 0.000000 595.275590551 841.88976378]
  /Type /Page
  /Contents [9 0 R]
>>
endobj
9 0 obj Content stream for page two
<< >>
stream
q 1. 0.000000 0.000000 1. 50. 770. cm BT /F0 36. Tf (Page Two) Tj ET Q
1. 0.000000 0.000000 1. 50. 750 cm BT /F0 16 Tf ((Rotated by 270 degrees)) Tj ET
endstream
endobj
7 0 obj Content stream for page three
<< >>
stream
1. 0.000000 0.000000 1. 50. 770. cm BT /F0 36. Tf (Page Three) Tj ET
endstream
endobj
10 0 obj Document information dictionary
<<
  /Title (PDF Explained Example)
  /Author (John Whitington)
  /Producer (Manually Created)
  /ModDate (D:201103130023467)
  /CreationDate (D:2011)
>>
endobj xref
0 11
trailer Trailer dictionary
<<
  /Info 10 0 R
  /Root 5 0 R
  /Size 11
  /ID [<75ff22189ceac848dfa2afec93deee03> <75ff22189ceac848dfa2afec93deee03>]
>>
startxref
0
%%EOF
```

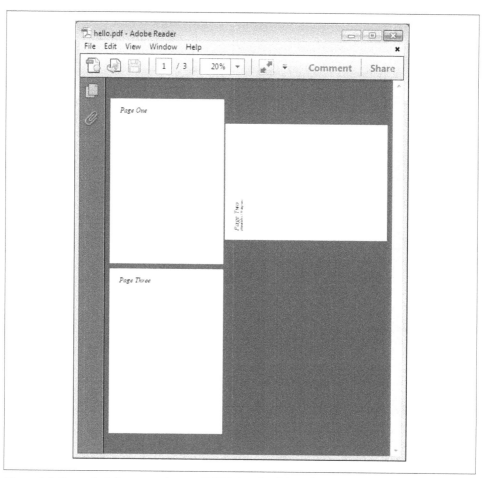

Figure 4-3. Example 4-3 converted to a valid PDF with pdftk and displayed in Acrobat Reader

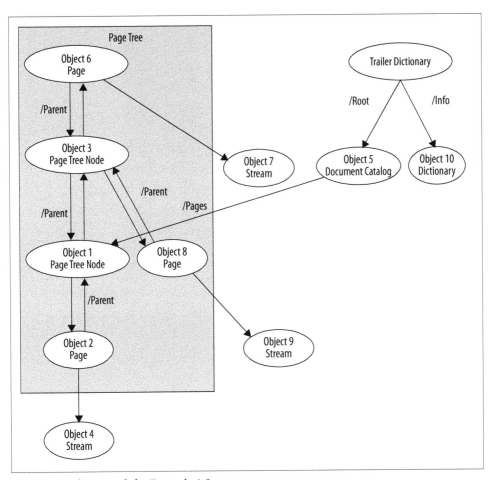

Figure 4-4. Object graph for Example 4-3

CHAPTER 5

Graphics

In this chapter, we'll run through the main ways to build graphics in the content stream of a PDF page. All of the examples are based on the same PDF we created manually in Chapter 2 and processed into valid PDF documents with *pdftk* in the same fashion. All the examples are included in the online resources.

Looking at Content Streams

A PDF page is made up of one or more *content streams*, defined by the /Contents entry in the page object, together with a shared set of resources, defined by the /Resources entry. In all our examples, there will only be a single content stream. Multiple content streams are equivalent to a single stream containing their concatenated content.

Here's an example page, with no resources and a single content stream:

```
3 0 obj
<<
  /Type /Page
  /Parent 1 0 R
  /Resources << >>
  /MediaBox [ 0 0 792 612 ]
  /Rotate 0
  /Contents [ 2 0 R ]
>>
endobj
```

Here's the associated content stream, consisting of the *stream dictionary* and the *stream data*.

```
2 0 obj
<< /Length 18 >> Stream dictionary
stream
200 150 m 600 450 l S Stream data
endstream
endobj
```

We'll discover what the m, l and S operators do in a moment. The numbers are measurements in *points*—a point (or pt) is 1/72 inch. The result of loading this document into a PDF viewer (after processing with *pdftk* as per Chapter 2) is shown in Figure 5-1.

The full manually created file (before processing with *pdftk*) is shown in Example 5-1. We're going to be using variations on this file for the rest of this chapter. For the most part we'll just change the content stream for each example, but later on we'll need to add one or more extra resources to the PDF. All of these files are found in the online resources for this book.

Example 5-1. Skeleton PDF listing for examples in this chapter

```
%PDF-1.1  PDF header
1 0 obj  Page tree
<< /Kids [2 0 R]
   /Type /Pages
   /Count 1
>>
endobj
2 0 obj  Page object
<< /Rotate 0
   /Parent 1 0 R
   /MediaBox [0 0 792 612]
   /Resources 3 0 R
   /Type /Page
   /Contents [4 0 R]
>>
endobj
3 0 obj  Resources
<< >>
4 0 obj  Page content stream
<< /Length 19 >>
stream
200 150 m 600 450 l S
endstream
endobj
5 0 obj  Document catalog
<< /Pages 1 0 R
   /Type /Catalog
>>
endobj xref  Skeleton cross-reference table
0 6
trailer  Trailer dictionary
<< /Root 5 0 R
   /Size 6
>>
startxref
0
%%EOF  End-of-file marker
```

Content streams are almost always compressed, so to inspect the content stream of an existing document, we can use the *pdftk* decompress operation. For example, the command:

```
pdftk input.pdf decompress output output.pdf
```

writes `input.pdf` to `output.pdf` with the streams uncompressed.

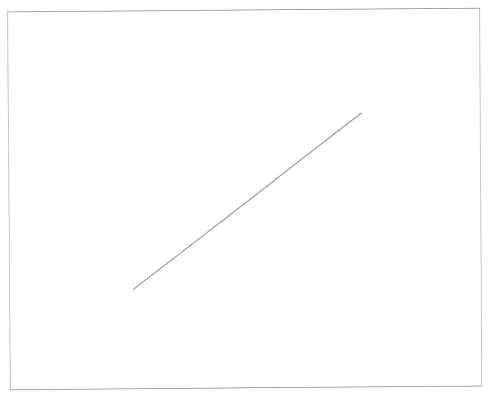

Figure 5-1. Defining and stroking a single line

Operators and Graphics State

A content stream consists of a series of *operators*, each preceded by zero or more *operands*. Table 5-1 lists the 78 graphics operators in 6 groups. In this chapter, we'll be looking at selected operators from the first four groups.

Table 5-1. PDF graphics operators

Group	Used for	Operators
Graphics state operators	Changing the graphics state (current color, stroke width etc).	w J j M d ri i gs q Q cm CS cs SC SCN sc scn G g RG rg K k
Path construction operators	Building lines, curves, and rectangles.	m l c v y h re
Path painting operators	Stroke and fill paths, or use them to define clipping regions.	S s f F f* B B* b b* n W W*

Group	Used for	Operators
Other painting operators	Shading patterns and inline images.	sh BI ID EI Do
Text operators	Select and show text in various fonts and ways.	Tc Tw Tz TL Tf Tr Ts Td TD Tm T* Tj TJ ' '' d0 d1
Marked content and compatibility operators	Used to demarcate sections of the stream.	MP DP BMC BDC EMC BX EX

The page is rendered by considering each operator and its operands in turn. The *graphics state* is maintained throughout, altered by some operators, consulted by others. Operands are often numbers, but can be names, dictionaries, or arrays.

The part of the graphics state which would be needed to render our examples, as it may appear in a typical PDF implementation, is summarized in Table 5-2.

Table 5-2. Graphics state

Entry	Type	Initial value
Current transformation matrix	matrix	The matrix which transforms default user coordinates to device coordinates
Fill color	color	Black
Line color	color	Black
Line width	real	1.0
Path join style	integer	Mitered joins (0)
Cap style	integer	Square butt caps (0)
Line dash pattern	integer array	Solid line
Current clipping path	path	The empty path
Blend mode	name or array	Normal
Soft mask	name or dictionary	None
Alpha constant	real	1.0 (full opacity)
Alpha source	boolean	false

Building and Painting Paths

We're using a landscape US Letter page (width 11 inches or 792 points; height 8.5 inches or 612 pts). The PDF coordinate system, by default, has the origin at the lower-left corner of the page, with *x* and *y* increasing rightward and upward, respectively.

Let's use some path construction, stroking, and line attribute operators to build a simple graphics stream:

```
100 100 m 300 200 l 700 100 l   Move to (100, 100), line to (300, 200), line to (700, 100)
S   Stroke the line
8 w   Change line width from the default (1.0) to 8.0
```

1 J *Change line ending cap to rounded (code 1) from default square (code 0)*
100 200 m 300 300 l 700 200 l *Define new path, same shape but 100pts higher up the page*
S *Stroke the new line*
[20] 0 d *Change to 20pt dashes*
100 300 m 300 400 l 700 300 l *Define new path, same shape but another 100pts higher up the page*
S *Stroke the new line*

The result is shown in Figure 5-2.

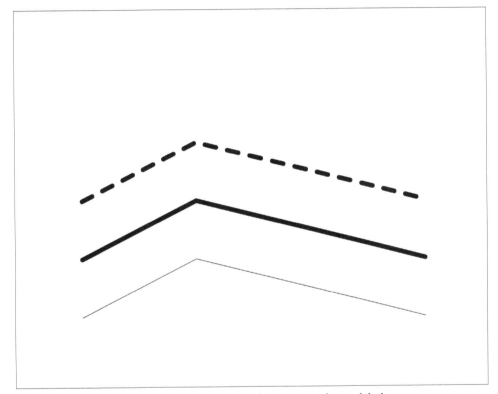

Figure 5-2. Building lines with differing widths, end caps, join styles, and dash patterns

We've used the m operator to move to the start of the new path, and the l operator to form two lines. Note that at this point, nothing has been drawn—the page is only affected when we use the S operator to stroke the line. The S operator also clears the current path.

The w operator sets the line width in the graphics state to 8 points. The J operator sets the line endings to rounded caps. The dash pattern is set with the d operator, which takes two operands: an array (which is a repeating sequence of dash length, gap length, dash length etc, which are cycled through when stroking the line), and an initial offset (the *phase*) which moves the start of the pattern. In our example, there is just one entry, so dashes and gaps are both 20pt, and the phase is 0.

Line joins, dash patterns, and line caps are summarized in Table 5-3, Table 5-4, and Table 5-5, respectively.

Paths may be made from more than one *subpath*, each subpath starting with the m operator. This can be used to define a single path made from several discontiguous shapes.

Table 5-3. Line joins

Join number	Meaning
0	Mitered join
1	Rounded join
2	Beveled join

Table 5-4. Dash patterns

Dash pattern specification	Meaning
[] 0	Solid line
[2] 0	2 on, 2 off, 2 on...
[2] 1	1 on, 2 off, 2 on... (phase is set to 1)
[2 3] 0	2 on, 3 off, 2 on...

Table 5-5. Line caps

Cap number	Meaning
0	Butt caps. Squared off at the end of the line.
1	Round caps. Semicircles attached at the end of each line.
2	Projecting square caps. Projects at end of line for half the width of the line, and is then squared off.

Bézier Curves

As well as straight lines, we can draw curves. There are many different possible schemes for defining curves, but the industry has settled on *Bézier* curves, named for the automobile engineer Pierre Bézier. They are easy and predictable to manipulate with the mouse onscreen, relatively easy to draw at any resolution or accuracy, and simple to define mathematically.

A curve is defined by four points—the start and end points, and two *control points* which define how the curve is shaped between start and end. The curve does not necessarily pass through the control points, but always sits fully inside the convex quadrilateral defined by its four points.

An example curve, showing the start and end points and the two control points (shown with dotted lines from the end points, as they may be represented in a graphics editor) can be seen in Figure 5-3.

This was generated by using the c operator:

```
300 200 m 400 300 500 400 600 200 c S
```

We use the m operator to move the current point to the start of the curve. The c operator takes three more coordinates: the first control point, second control point, and end point.

For more information on Bézier curves, consult a graphics text—see "PDF and Graphics Documentation" on page 119.

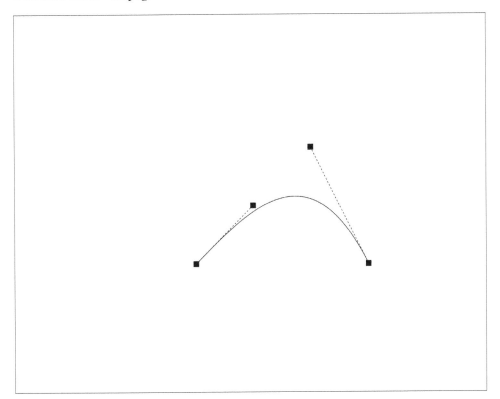

Figure 5-3. A Bézier curve

Drawing circles with Bézier curves

Interestingly, it's not possible to draw exact circles in PDF. But we can use several Bézier curves to approximate one closely. We'll use four symmetric curves (the minimum number to get a good result), one for each quadrant. For a specimen quadrant of the unit circle centered at (1, 0), the coordinates are shown in Figure 5-4. The number k is about 0.552.

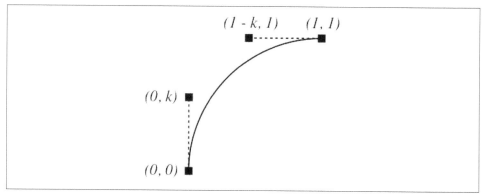

Figure 5-4. Approximating a circular arc with a Bézier curve

Filled Shapes and Winding Rules

Paths may be filled as well as stroked, by substituting another operator from Table 5-6 for the S operation we used before (here, we used B to fill and stroke the path). Figure 5-5 shows a shape filled and stroked using the following code:

```
2.0 w
0.75 g Change fill color to light Gray
250 250 m Move to start of path
350 350 450 450 550 250 c First curve
450 250 350 200 y Second curve
h B Close and fill
```

We've used the g operator to set the fill color. This is explained in "Colors and Color Spaces" on page 60. For the second curve, we've used the y operator which is like c, except that the second control point and the end point are one and the same, so only four operands are needed.

There are two factors distinguishing fill operators from one another:

- Whether the path is automatically *closed* before filling. Closing involves adding a straight line segment from the current point to the starting point of the current subpath. The path may be manually closed with the h operator.
- The *winding rule* which determines the choices made when filling an object which is self-intersecting or made up of multiple subpaths which overlap. Figure 5-6 shows the effect of the two winding rules on both a self-intersecting object, and a path made from two overlapping rectangular subpaths.

The code for Figure 5-6 is:

```
100 350 200 200 re
120 370 160 160 re f Non-zero
400 350 200 200 re
420 370 160 160 re f* Even-odd
```

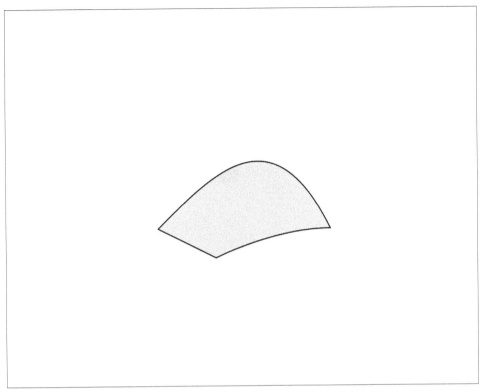

Figure 5-5. A filled shape

```
150 50 m 150 250 l 250 50 l 50 150 l 350 150 l h f
550 50 m 550 250 l 650 50 l 450 150 l 750 150 l h f*
```

Here, we've also used the re operator. This creates a rectangular, closed path given four arguments: minimum *x*, minimum *y*, width, and height.

Table 5-6. Operators for filling and stroking paths

Operator	Function
n	Ends the path with no visual effect. This is used to change the current clipping path (see "Clipping" on page 65).
b	Close, fill and stroke the path (non-zero winding rule)
b*	Close, fill and stroke the path (even-odd winding rule)
B	Fill and stroke the path (non-zero winding rule)
B*	Fill and stroke the path (even-odd winding rule)
f or F	Fill the path (non-zero winding rule)
f*	Fill the path (even-odd winding rule)
S	Stroke the path
s	Close and stroke the path

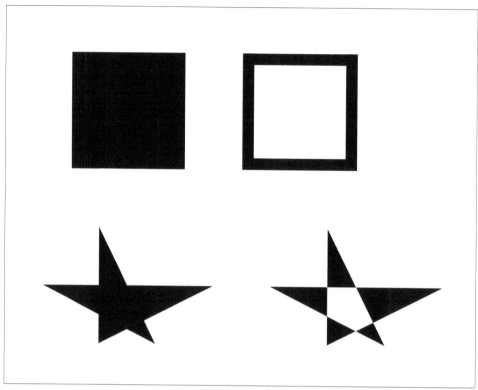

Figure 5-6. Non-zero (L) and even-odd (R) winding rules

Colors and Color Spaces

To change the fill or stroke color in a PDF graphics stream, we need to change the current color space using one operator, and then change the color using another. Fill and stroke color spaces are separate—the current fill color space could be *DeviceRGB* and the stroke color space *DeviceGray*, for example.

In this section, we look at the basic *DeviceGray*, *DeviceRGB*, and *DeviceCMYK* color spaces (more complicated color spaces are covered in the PDF Standard):

- The *DeviceGray* color space has one additive component, which varies from 0.0 (Black) to 1.0 (White).

- The *DeviceRGB* color space has three additive components for Red, Green, and Blue. They each range from 0.0 (e.g., no Red) to 1.0 (e.g., full Red).

- The *DeviceCMYK* color space has four subtractive components for Cyan, Magenta, Yellow, and Key (Black). They each range from 0.0 (no pigment) to 1.0 (full pigment).

To change the stroke color space, we use the CS operator. To change the fill color space, use cs instead. The SC operator (with a number of operands equal to the number of components in the current color space) can then be used to set the stroke color, or sc to set the fill color. For example:

```
/DeviceRGB CS Set stroke color space
0.0 0.5 0.9 SC Set color to RGB (0.0, 0.5, 0.9)
```

There are shortcut operators for the device color spaces, which set the current stroke or fill color space and the current stroke or fill color in one operation. These are summarized in Table 5-7.

Table 5-7. Simple color and color space operators

Operator	Operands	Function
G	1	Change stroke color space to /DeviceGray and set color
g	1	Change fill color space to /DeviceGray and set color
RG	3 (R, G, B)	Change stroke color space to /DeviceRGB and set color
rg	3 (R, G, B)	Change fill color space to /DeviceRGB and set color
K	4 (C, M, Y, K)	Change stroke color space to /DeviceCMYK and set color
k	4 (C, M, Y, K)	Change fill color space to /DeviceCMYK and set color

When a content stream begins, the default color space is /DeviceGray and the default color value is 0 (fully black), so we can use the re operator straight away:

```
200 250 100 100 re f
0.25 g
300 250 100 100 re f
0.5 g
400 250 100 100 re f
0.75 g
500 250 100 100 re f
```

The result is shown in Figure 5-7.

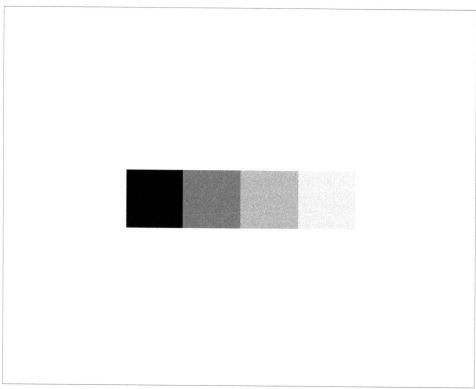

Figure 5-7. The DeviceGray color space

Transformations

So far, we've seen operators that alter the graphics state of all the operators that follow them. In order to allow us to group together graphics objects with their attributes (such as color), we can bracket a group of operators with the q and Q operators. The q operator puts aside the current graphics state. The state may then be altered, objects painted, and so on— as usual. When the Q operator is invoked, the previous saved state is restored. The q/Q pairs may be nested, one pair inside another:

```
0.75 g  Change to light Gray fill
250 250 100 100 re f
q  Save the graphics state
0.25 g  Change to dark Gray fill
350 250 100 100 re f
Q  Retrieve the previous graphics state
450 250 100 100 re f  Light Gray again
```

The q/Q operators in a stream must form balanced pairs (with the exception that, at the end of a graphics stream, any remaining Q operators may be omitted). The result is shown in Figure 5-8.

Figure 5-8. Using q and Q operators to isolate color attributes

One of the most frequent uses of q/Q pairs is to isolate the effects of *coordinate transforms*. We can use the cm operator to change the transformation from *user space coordinates* to *device space coordinates*. This is known as the *Current Transformation Matrix* (CTM). It's important that this change to the graphics state is isolated by a q/Q pair, because it's complicated to undo.

The cm operator takes six arguments, representing a matrix to be composed with the CTM. Here are the basic transforms:

- Translation by *(dx, dy)* is specified by *1, 0, 0, 1, dx, dy*
- Scaling by *(sx, sy)* about *(0, 0)* is specified by *sx, 0, 0, sy, 0, 0*
- Rotating counterclockwise by *x* radians about *(0, 0)* is specified by *cos x, sin x, -sin x, cos x, 0, 0*

The cm operator appends the given transform to the CTM, rather than replacing it. To rotate or scale around an arbitrary point (rather than the origin), translate to the origin, rotate or scale, and translate back.

Any graphics text will have a full discussion of the mathematics of such transforms. See "PDF and Graphics Documentation" on page 119.

Consider the following, illustrated in Figure 5-9:

```
2.0 w
0.75 g
100 100 m 200 200 300 300 400 100 c  (a) Untransformed shape
300 100 200 50 y h B
q
0.96 0.25 -0.25 0.96 0 0 cm   (b) Rotate counterclockwise by 1/4 radian
100 100 m 200 200 300 300 400 100 c
300 100 200 50 y h B
Q
q
0.5 0 0 0.5 0 0 cm  (c) Scale original shape by 0.5 about the origin
100 100 m 200 200 300 300 400 100 c
300 100 200 50 y h B
1 0 0 1 300 0 cm  (d) Translate (c) by 300 units in the new space, i.e., 150 units in the original space
100 100 m 200 200 300 300 400 100 c
300 100 200 50 y h B
Q
```

Note the use of q and Q to isolate the effect of transforms.

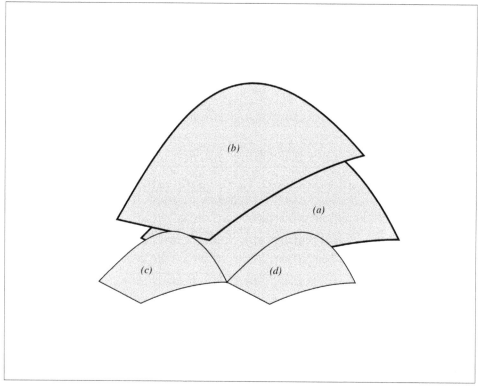

Figure 5-9. Translation, scaling and rotation with the cm operator

Clipping

We can use a path, built in the usual way, to set the *clipping path*. From that point on, only content within the path's area will be shown. This is done by using the W operator (for a non-zero path) or W* operator (for an even-odd path).

The operator intersects the path given with the existing clipping path, so it can only be used to make the clipping region smaller, not larger. The clipping path remains the current path, so it can be used to stroke the outline of the clipping region using, for example, the S operator. The W operator is a modifier to the painting operation, so if we don't want to stroke the outline of the new clipping path, we must substitute the no-op path painting operator n. Here's an example where we define a clipping path:

```
200 100 m 200 500 l 500 100 l h W S
```

Here we have defined a closed triangular path, set the clipping region using W and then stroked it using S. The result of setting this clipping path and then drawing the same scene as Figure 5-2 can be seen in Figure 5-10.

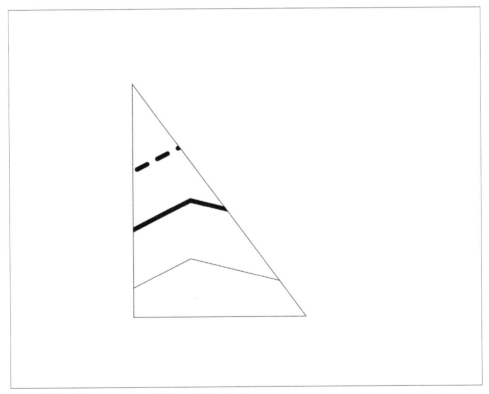

Figure 5-10. Clipping to a path (the path is also shown)

Transparency

PDF has a sophisticated but complicated transparency mechanism which works in multiple color spaces, allows different types of blending, and supports grouped transparencies. We only consider simple transparency here.

There are no specific transparency operators so we use the gs operator to load the fill transparency level from the /ca entry in the /ExtGState entry in the page's resources. The /ExtGState entry is a dictionary of collections of *external graphics state*, which we can load in using the gs operator.

For our example, the resources consist of just the /ExtGState entry, with a single collection of state, called /gs1. It contains just the /ca entry for fill transparency:

```
<< /ExtGState
  << /gs1
    << /ca 0.5 >> Half transparent
  >>
>>
```

Here is the corresponding content stream:

```
2.0 w Select 2pt line width
/gs1 gs Select /gs1 from external graphics state
0.75 g Select light Gray
200 250 m 300 350 400 450 500 250 c
400 250 300 200 y h B
1 0 0 1 100 100 cm
200 250 m 300 350 400 450 500 250 c
400 250 300 200 y h B
```

The result is shown in Figure 5-11. The transparency is defined so that 0 means wholly transparent, and 1 wholly opaque. The stroke transparency may be altered with /CA in place of (or in addition to) /ca.

Shadings and Patterns

As well as plain colors, PDF allows various *patterns* to be used to fill and stroke objects:

- *Tiling patterns*, where a *pattern cell* is replicated over the page.
- *Shading patterns*, where a gradient between colors is used to fill an object. There are many types, with many options and settings:

> Function-based
> Axial
> Radial
> Free-form Gouraud-shaded triangle mesh
> Lattice-form Gouraud-shaded triangle mesh
> Coons patch mesh
> Tensor-product patch mesh

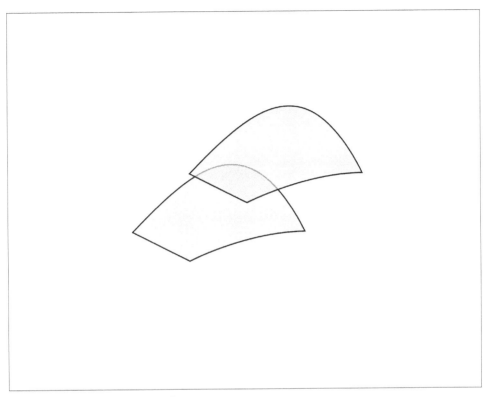

Figure 5-11. Transparency in PDF

We consider just Axial and Radial shadings.

Patterns are invoked by changing to the /Pattern color space using the cs operator, then using the scn operator to select a named pattern. Patterns are listed by name in the /Pattern dictionary in the page's resources. For example:

```
/Pattern
  <<
    /GradientShading  Our name for the pattern
    <<
      /Type /Pattern
      /PatternType 2  A shading pattern
      /Shading
        <<
          /ColorSpace /DeviceGray
          /ShadingType 2  An axial shading
          /Function << /FunctionType 2 /N 1 /Domain [0 1] >>
          /Coords [150 200 450 500]  Coordinates of start and end of gradient
          /Extend [true true]
        >>
    >>
  >>
```

This defines an axial shading pattern. We have named our pattern /GradientShading. The pattern type for shadings is 2. Our shading is defined by:

- The color space /DeviceGray
- The shading type 2 (Axial)
- The coordinates of the start and end of the shading: (150, 200) and (450, 500)

We don't discuss the /Extend or /Function entries here. The pattern is now invoked, and a shape drawn:

```
/Pattern cs  Choose pattern color space for fills
/GradientShading scn  Choose our pattern as a color
250 300 m 350 400 450 500 550 300 c
450 300 350 250 y h f
```

The result is Figure 5-12.

Figure 5-12. An axial shading pattern

If we change to a radial shading by changing the /ShadingType to 3, and change the /Coords entry to [400 400 0 400 400 200]—a radial shading with inner radius 0 and outer radius 200 both centered on (400, 400):

```
/Coords [400 400 0 400 400 200]
/ShadingType 3
```

The result is shown in Figure 5-13.

Figure 5-13. A radial shading pattern

Form XObjects

In "Transformations" on page 62, we used the q and Q operators to display a single object using various transformations. However, we had to recite the operations for drawing the object each time. A *Form XObject* allows us to store a set of graphics instructions, and use them repeatedly (even on different pages), at differing scales and positions.

 Form XObjects have nothing to do with PDF forms (the kind you fill in).

```
3 0 obj  Resources of current page
<<
   /XObject << /X1 5 0 R >>  Our XObject is called /X1
>>
endobj
5 0 obj  The XObject itself
<<  The XObject dictionary
   /Type /XObject
   /Subtype /Form
   /Length 69
   /BBox [0 0 792 612]
>>
stream  The XObject content
2.0 w
0.5 g
250 300 m 350 400 450 500 500 300 c
450 300 350 250 y h B
endstream
endobj
```

Object 3 in the listing above is the page's /Resources entry. Its /XObject entry is a dictionary listing the XObjects used in that page. We've named our XObject /X1. Object 5 is the XObject itself. It's a stream, with the following entries in its dictionary:

- The /Type of this object is /XObject.
- The /Subtype of this XObject is /Form, distinguishing it as a form XObject.
- The /Length is the length in bytes of the stream, as usual.
- The /BBox entry gives a bounding box for the XObject, in this case the same as the page itself.

The stream contains the code for setting up the line and width, and the shape itself. Now, we can use the XObject from the main content stream, using the Do operator with the XObject's name as the operand:

```
/X1 Do  Invoke XObject /X1
0.5 0 0 0.5 0 0 cm  Scale by 0.5 about the origin
/X1 Do  Invoke the XObject again, at the new scale
```

The result is shown in Figure 5-14.

When the Do operator is encountered, the current graphics state is saved, the /Matrix entry (if any) from the XObject is concatenated with the CTM, the content is drawn (clipped by the XObject's /BBox), and the current graphics state is restored.

Image XObjects

Images are specified using separate objects, again stored in the /XObject entry in the page's resources dictionary. They are thus separate from the graphics content stream, and so may be reused multiple times, even across pages. To specify an image, we provide the image data (usually compressed using one of many mechanisms such as JPEG), its

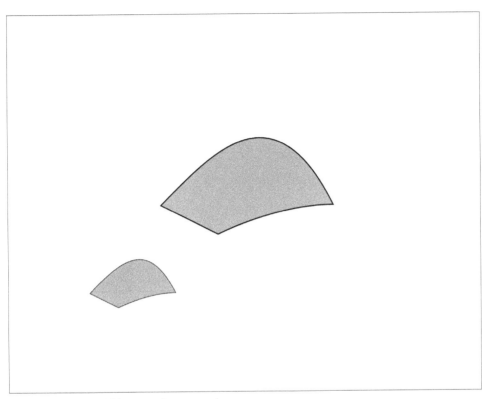

Figure 5-14. Form XObject used at two scales

width and height, and some parameters which describe the conversion from the image data to values in its color space.

Here is a resources entry for an image XObject:

```
<< /XObject << /X2 5 0 R >> >>
```

This defines an image XObject called **/X2** whose parameters are:

```
5 0 obj
<<
  /Type /XObject   It's an XObject
  /Subtype /Image   It's an image
  /ColorSpace /DeviceGray   The color space of the image. Also determines how many components it has.
  /Length 8   The length of the stream in bytes, as usual
  /Width 8   Image width in pixels
  /Height 8   Image height in pixels
  /BitsPerComponent 1   Number of bits used for each component
>>
stream
@`pxxp`@   The image data
endstream
```

To make this possible to type in manually, we've defined a one-bit-per-pixel black and white image, containing just 64 bits of data. Typically, images would be hundreds or thousands of pixels in each direction and with up to 16 bits per component, with one, three, or four components.

Images always map to the square *(0,0)…(1,1)* in user space, so we use cm operators to scale the image to the appropriate size and position:

```
q
1 0 0 1 100 100 cm Translate
200 0 0 200 0 0 cm Scale
/X2 Do Invoke image XObject
Q
q
1 0 0 1 400 100 cm And again with a different position and scale
100 0 0 100 0 0 cm
/X2 Do
Q
```

The result is shown in Figure 5-15.

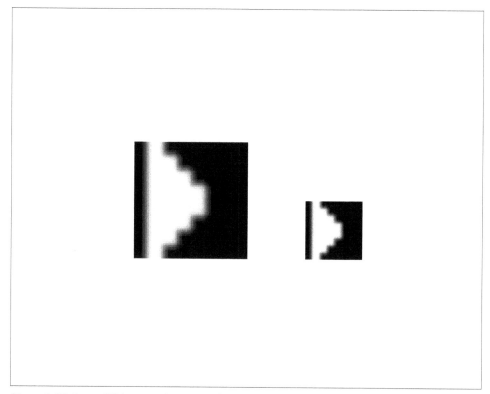

Figure 5-15. Image XObject used at two scales

CHAPTER 6

Text and Fonts

In the previous chapter, we saw how a series of graphics operators can be used to draw content on a page, by reference to their operands and a stack-based graphics state.

In this chapter, we look at the operators and state for selecting characters from fonts and printing them on the page. Then, we see how fonts and their metrics are defined and embedded in PDF documents. Finally, we discuss the complex task of general-purpose text extraction from a document.

Text and Fonts in PDF

It would be possible to define a page description language where none of the text layout had been performed, and plain text was supplied along with boxes and columns to be filled on-the-fly, just like a desktop publishing package. Conversely, it would be possible to define a page description language without fonts or text as such at all, just relying on text being converted to outline shapes as the document is produced, having been layed out in, for example, a word-processor.

PDF adopts a middle ground—the ideas of a font and of small-scale text layout are retained, but the large-scale paragraph layout must be done in advance. This has the following advantages:

- Complete control over layout, because large-scale layout (paragraphs, line-breaks) are the job of the program producing the PDF. The document will look as it is supposed to.

- Predictable small-scale text layout, such as fixed character spacing, is supported, so the position of each character need not be explicitly stated.

- Space saved by the use of fonts as libraries of character shapes, and the simple inclusion of existing font files minimizing compatibility and portability problems.

- Original characters and some layout elements are maintained, so copy-and-paste and text extraction are normally possible.

Text State

The text state parameters and the operators which modify them are summarized in Table 6-1.

Table 6-1. Text state parameters and their operators

Parameter	Description	Operands	Operators	Initial value
T_c	Character spacing	charSpace	Tc sets the character spacing to *charSpace*, expressed in unscaled text space units.	0
T_w	Word spacing	wordSpace	Tw sets the word spacing to *wordSpace*, expressed in unscaled text units.	0
T_h	Horizontal spacing	scale	Tz sets the horizontal scaling to (*scale* / 100).	100 (normal spacing)
T_l	Leading	leading	TL sets the text leading to *leading*, expressed in unscaled text space units.	0
T_f, T_{fs}	Font, Font Size	font, size	Tf selects the font *font* at size *size* points.	None. Must be specified.
T_{mode}	Rendering Mode	render	Tr sets the text rendering mode to *render*, an integer.	0
T_{rise}	Rise	rise	Ts sets the text rise to *rise*, expressed in unscaled text space units.	0

We discuss the phrase "unscaled text space units" in "Text Space and Text Positioning" on page 75. The text state is stored along with the graphics state, and manipulated using the operators above. The current text state is affected by the stack operators q and Q, just like the graphics state.

Printing Text

Printing text on the page requires:

1. Selecting a font.
2. Choosing position, size, and orientation.
3. Choosing spacing, color, text rendering mode, and other parameters.
4. Selecting characters from the font, and showing them on the page.

Text Sections

The operators BT (begin text) and ET (end text) form brackets around *text sections*. Operators for showing text in a page's content stream may only appear between BT and ET. Operators for altering text state, however, are not restricted in this way. Text sections may also contain other operators altering the general graphics state.

As an example, we return to the "Hello, World!" file from Chapter 2:

```
1. 0. 0. 1. 50. 700. cm Position at (50, 700)
BT  Begin text block
  /F0 36. Tf Select /F0 font at 36pt
  (Hello, World!) Tj Place the text string
ET End text block
```

Here, we've used the Tf operator with font name and size operators to select the font, and the Tj operator to show a text string. We have relied on the graphics operator cm to position the text. Now, we will discuss other methods of changing the text position.

Text Space and Text Positioning

Text space is the coordinate system in which text is defined. The transformation from this text space into user space (and then into device space, as usual) determines where text is placed on the page. The origin of the first glyph in the text string is placed at the origin of text space.

There are two matrices to consider:

- The *text matrix*, which defines the current transformation for the next glyph. It is altered by the text positioning and text showing operators.
- The *text line matrix*, which is the state of the text matrix at the beginning of the current line. Thus, lines of text may be aligned vertically by the use of an operator to move to the next line, without manually keeping track of the position of the start of the line.

These matrices do not persist from text section to text section, but are reset to the identity matrix at the beginning of each text section. Together with the font size, horizontal scaling, and text rise, these two matrices define the transformation from text space to user space.

The operators for modifying the text position are summarized in Table 6-2.

Table 6-2. Operators for positioning text

Operands	Operator	Function
x,y	Td	Move the text position to the next line, offset by (x,y). The parameters are expressed in unscaled text space units.
x,y	TD	Move the text position to the next line, offset by (x,y). Sets the leading to -y. The parameters are expressed in unscaled text space units.
-	T*	Move the text position to the next line. Equivalent to the sequence 0 *leading* Td (where *leading* is the current text leading).
a,b,c,d,e,f	Tm	Sets the text matrix and text line matrix to [a b 0 c d 0 e f 1]. Unlike the graphics matrix operator cm, the matrix replaces the current matrix, rather than being concatenated with it.

Showing Text

The Tj operator shows text at the current position. This, in combination with the text positioning operators we have already seen would suffice. However, for convenience and brevity, three additional operators (', '', and TJ) are provided. These are shortcuts for common combinations of text-showing and text-positioning. The text showing operators are summarized in Table 6-3.

Table 6-3. Operators for showing text

Operands	Operator	Function
string	Tj	Show *string* at the current position.
string	'	Go to the next line, taking into account the leading and text matrices, and show *string* at the new position. The same as using T* followed by Tj.
wordspace, charspace, string	''	Set the word spacing to *wordspace* and the character spacing to *charspace*. Go to the next line, taking into account the leading and text matrices, and show *string* at the new position. The same the sequence *wordspace* Tw *charspace* Tc *string* '.
array	TJ	This operator allows a text string to be shown with adjustments for individual glyph positions (for example, kerning). The array contains strings and numbers, in any combination. String entries are shown as normal; number entries adjust the text matrix horizontally by subtracting that amount (expressed in thousandths of a unit of text space).

We will now go through some examples of showing text, using the standard fonts and PDFDocEncoding for simplicity. As always, these examples can be found in the online resources.

Character and word spacing

Here is our first example, where we show some lines of text using various operators. The result is illustrated in Figure 6-1:

```
BT
/F0 36 Tf
1 0 0 1 120 350 Tm
50 TL
(Character and Word Spacing) Tj T*
3 Tc
(Character and Word Spacing) Tj T*
10 Tw
(Character and Word Spacing) Tj
ET
```

In this example we have:

1. Used Tf to select font /F0 at 36 points.
2. Used Tm to set the text position to (120, 350).
3. Used TL to set the leading to 50 points.
4. Shown a string with Tj, and used T* to move to the next line.

5. Set the character spacing to 3 points, and drawn the string again.

6. Set the word spacing to 10 points, and drawn the string a third time.

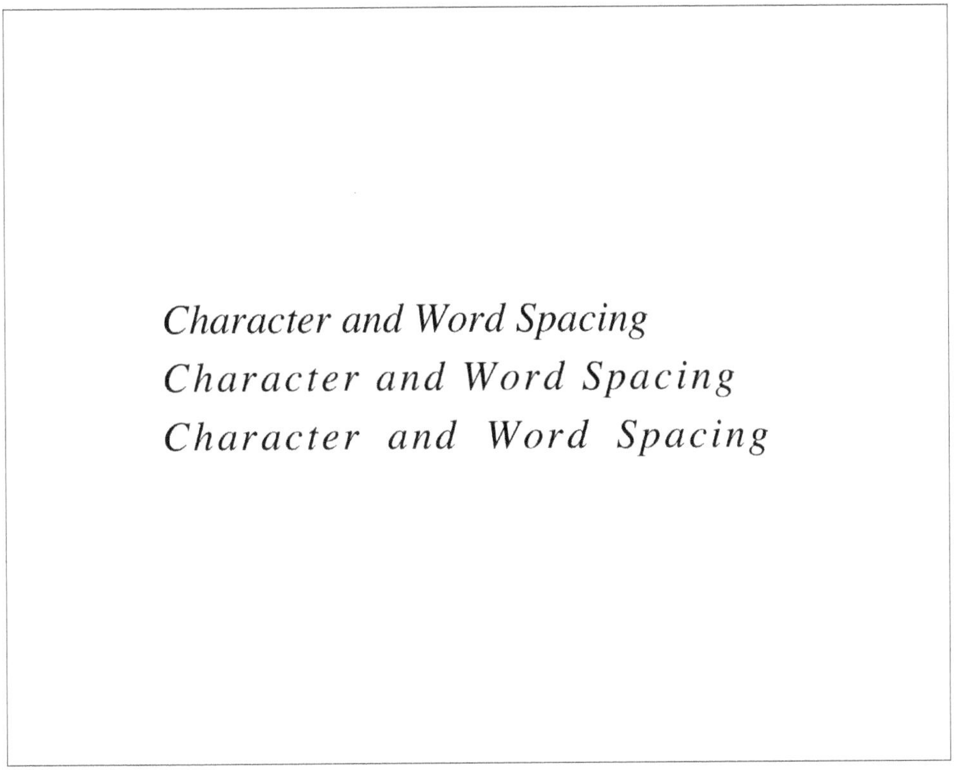

Character and Word Spacing

Character and Word Spacing

Character and Word Spacing

Figure 6-1. Character and word spacing

Text transforms

In this example, we show how text transforms combine with graphics transforms to make sure that text positioning operations (for example, moving to the next line) work properly, even when the whole text section is transformed. The result is Figure 6-2:

```
0.96 0.25 -0.25 0.96 0 0 cm
BT
/F0 48 Tf
48 TL
1 0 0 1 270 240 Tm
(Text and graphics) Tj T*
(transforms combined) Tj T*
(with newlines) Tj
ET
```

Here, we have:

1. Set up the graphics matrix to rotate anticlockwise around the origin with cm.
2. Selected a font and set the leading with Tf and TL.
3. Set the text matrix to offset the start by (270, 240) with Tm.
4. Written three lines with Tj and T*.

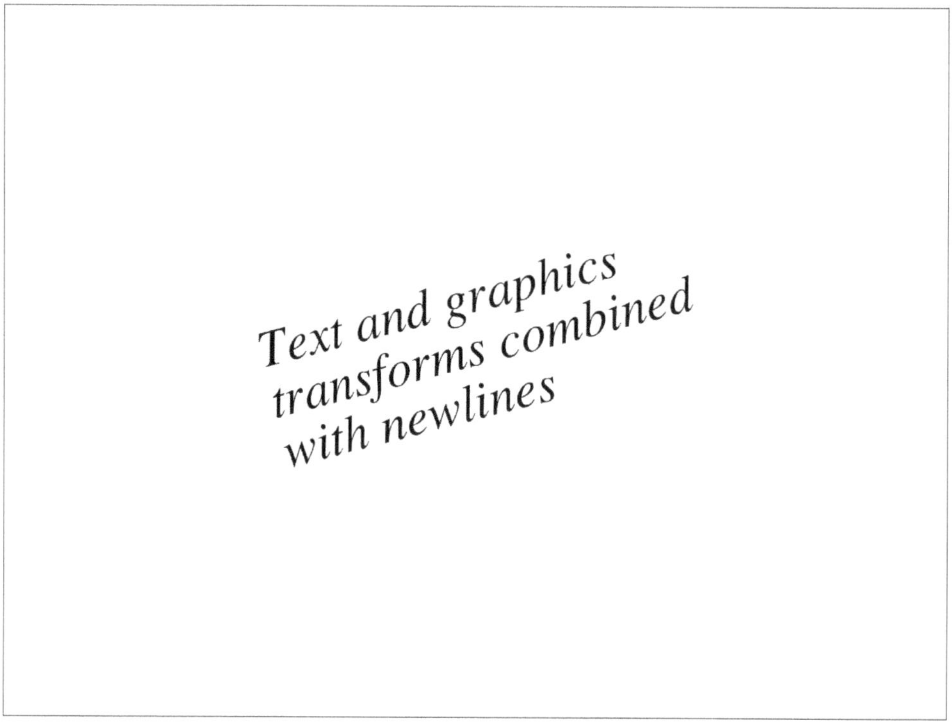

Figure 6-2. Text transforms

Text rise

The Ts operator can be used to adjust the vertical position of text:

```
BT
/F0 72 Tf
1 0 0 1 140 290 Tm
(Text) Tj
20 Ts
(Up) Tj
0 Ts
(and) Tj
-20 Ts
(Down) Tj
ET
```

The result is shown in Figure 6-3. This is the first time we've used multiple Tj operators without starting a new line. Note that the Tj operator, having shown the text, sets the text position to the end of the string which was just drawn.

Figure 6-3. Superscripting and subscripting with the text rise operator

Kerning and glyph adjustment

The TJ operator is an alternative to Tj for drawing a string with horizontal glyph adjustments. These typically occur when text is layed out in a word-processor or typesetter, especially if the content is fully justified. The TJ operator is a convenient way to encode this information without using dozens of operators for each line of text:

```
BT
/F0 72 Tf
90 TL
1 0 0 1 240 330 Tm
[(PJ WAYNE)] TJ T*
[(P)150(J )(W)150(A)80(YN)20(E)] TJ
ET
```

We have used TJ twice here; once to show the text as normal, and a second time including manual kerns in the array passed to TJ. The result is illustrated in Figure 6-4.

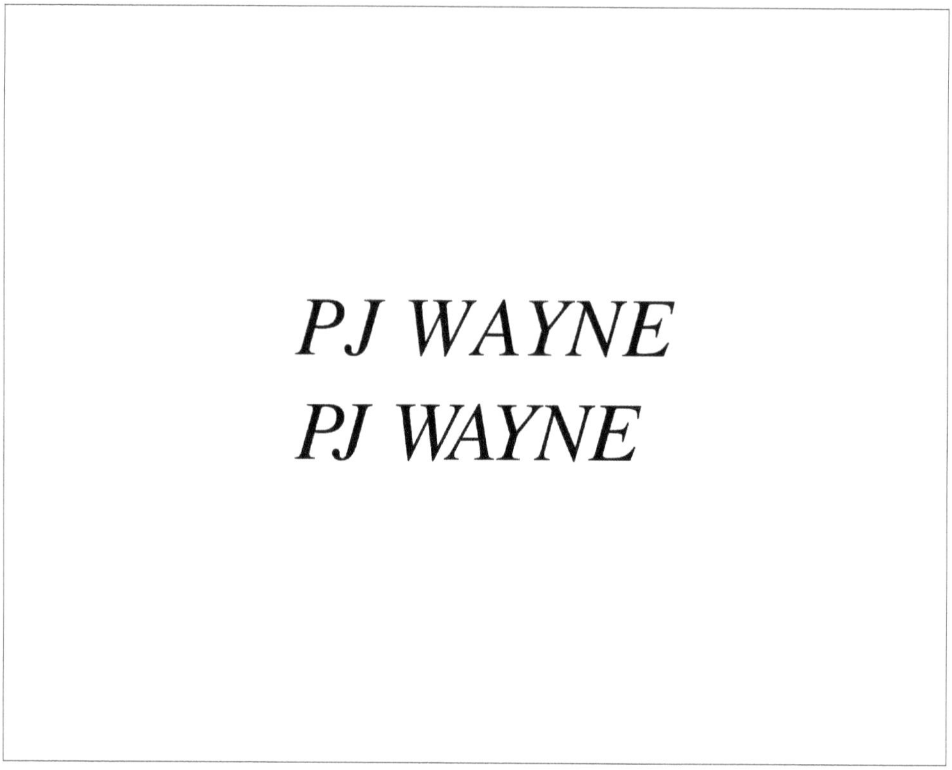

Figure 6-4. Kerned text

Text rendering modes

There are seven rendering modes for text, set with the Tr operator. Four of them are for setting up text as a clipping path, and one is for writing invisible text. We don't consider those here. The other three (modes 0, 1, and 2) are used for filling, stroking, and filling-followed-by-stroking respectively. The colors set in the same way as for shape drawing:

```
0.5 g
BT
/F0 72 Tf
1 0 0 1 160 380 Tm
90 TL
(Text Mode Zero) Tj T*
1 Tr
(Text Mode One) Tj T*
2 Tr
(Text Mode Two) Tj
ET
```

The result is illustrated in Figure 6-5.

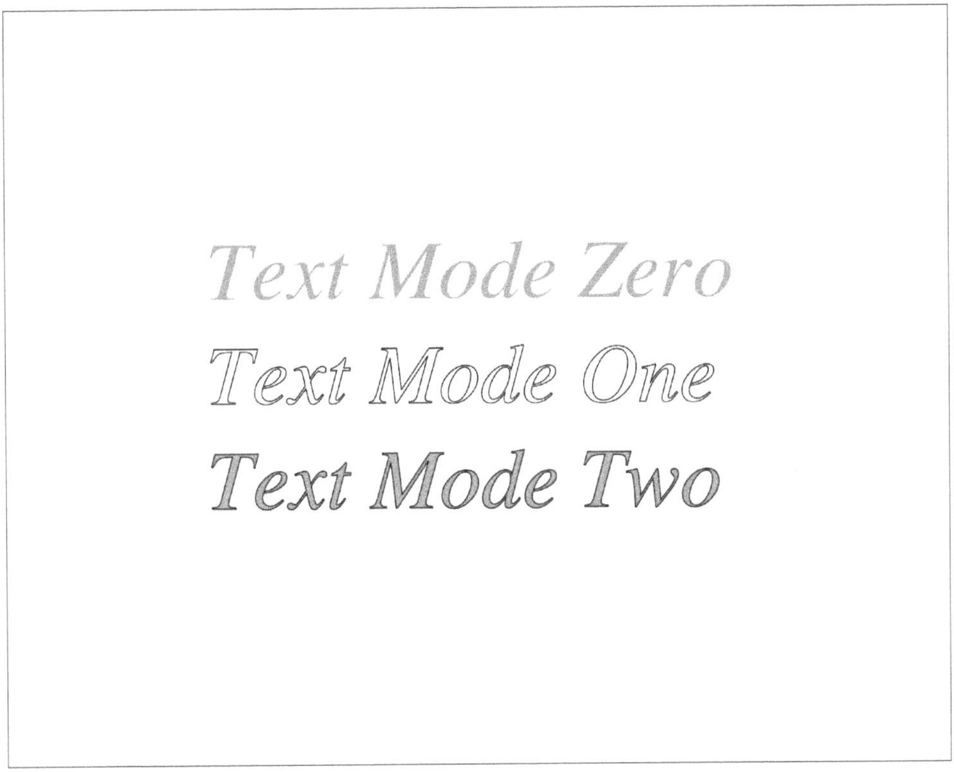

Figure 6-5. The simple text rendering modes

Defining and Embedding Fonts

A *font* is a collection of *glyphs* (character shapes) for a particular *character set*. In PDF, a font is composed of a *font dictionary* which defines the metrics, character set, and encoding (mapping of character codes in text strings to characters in the font), together with the *font program* (which is the actual font file), in a variety of formats (Type 1, TrueType etc).

Font Types in PDF

PDF allows the use of the major popular font formats, together with *Type 3 fonts* which allow the encoding of any other font type (for example, legacy bitmap fonts) by defining the character shapes directly using a collection of PDF graphics operators.

Type 1 fonts

Introduced with font type /Type1 in the font dictionary. Type 1 is an Adobe font format originally for use with PostScript. The standard 14 fonts are defined as Type 1 fonts. Multiple Master Type 1 fonts (/MMType1) are an extension of Type 1 allowing the automatic generation of many font styles from a one set of outlines.

TrueType fonts

Introduced with font type /TrueType in the font dictionary. Based on Apple's True-Type font format (also frequently used in Microsoft Windows).

Type 3 fonts

Introduced with font type /Type3. These are fonts composed of streams of PDF graphics operators. This means they can include colors and shadings, so are more flexible, but have no hinting mechanisms for clear display at small sizes. Often used to emulate other font formats (for example, bitmap fonts).

CID fonts

These are *composite fonts*, intended to support multibyte character sets (where a font has a huge number of glyphs, such as Chinese). They are not discussed in this text.

OpenType fonts

The OpenType font format is modeled after TrueType, but can also contain glyph descriptions in Type 1 format. It has support for fonts with a large number of glyphs, including mechanisms for ligature management and other advanced features.

Type 1 Fonts

We will use Type 1 fonts as an example. Table 6-4 summarizes the entries in a Type 1 font dictionary.

*Table 6-4. Type 1 font dictionary (*denotes required entry, **denotes required except for the standard 14 fonts)*

Key	Value type	Value
/Type*	name	Must be /Font.
/Subtype*	name	Must be /Type1.
/BaseFont*	name	The PostScript name for the font.
/FirstChar**	integer	The first code in the /Widths array.
/LastChar**	integer	The last code in the /Widths array.
/Widths**	array of integers	Array of length (/LastChar - /FirstChar + 1), giving the glyph width for those characters in thousandths of text space units.
/FontDescriptor**	indirect reference to dictionary	A *font descriptor dictionary* giving the font's metrics (other than the glyph widths).

Key	Value type	Value
/Encoding	name or dictionary	The font's character encoding, for example /MacRomanEncoding or /WinAnsiEncoding. More complicated ones are described by dictionaries.
/ToUnicode	stream	A stream containing instructions for the extraction of text content. See "Extracting Text from a Document" on page 86.

There are 14 standard Type 1 fonts in PDF. These are fonts where the metrics and outlines (or suitable substitution fonts) must be available in any PDF application. Nowadays, however, Adobe recommends that all fonts are fully embedded, even these. The standard fonts are:

Times-Roman
Times-Bold
Times-Italic
Times-BoldItalic
Helvetica
Helvetica-Bold
Helvetica-Oblique
Helvetica-BoldOblique
Courier
Courier-Bold
Courier-Oblique
Courier-BoldOblique
Symbol
ZapfDingbats

For example, here is a simple Type 1 font:

```
1 0 obj
<< /Type /Font
   /Subtype /Type1
   /BaseFont /Times-Roman
   /FirstChar 0
   /LastChar 255
   /Widths [ 255 255 255 255 ... 744 268 380 380 380 380 380 380 380 380 380 380 ]
   /FontDescriptor 2 0 R
   /Encoding /WinAnsiEncoding
>>
```

The ellipsis ... is content we have omitted, not part of the PDF language. We discuss the /FontDescriptor and /Encoding entries later. The /Widths array gives the widths in thousandths of a text space unit for each of the 256 characters in this font.

Font Encodings

The *font encoding* describes the mapping between character codes (characters in the strings used in content streams) and glyph descriptions in the font. Font programs have their own built-in encodings, but the PDF font can alter the encoding to use a Macintosh font with a Microsoft Windows encoding, or to use a single-byte encoding to select up to 256 characters from a font with more than 256 glyphs (e.g., variations on characters or ligatures).

The simplest /Encoding entry is just the name of one of the standard encodings, which are defined in the PDF Standard, Appendix D. More complicated encodings are defined by using a dictionary instead of a name for the encoding. The entries in this dictionary are summarized in Table 6-5.

Table 6-5. Entries in an encoding dictionary

Key	Value type	Value
/Type	name	Must be /Encoding
/BaseEncoding	name	The *base encoding*, from which the /Differences entry defines differences. This is one of the predefined encodings /MacRomanEncoding, /MacExpertEncoding, or /WinAnsiEncoding. If this entry is absent, the differences are from the font file's built-in encoding.
/Differences	array of integers and names	Defines the differences from the base encoding. Contains zero or more sections each beginning with a number *n* followed by glyph names for character n, n+1, n+2 etc. For example [6 /endash /emdash 34 /space] maps 6 to /endash, 7 to /emdash, and 34 to /space.

In Example 6-1, the font has an encoding that defines a difference from the built-in font encoding by replacing character 1 by the character /bullet (the bullet point). This means that the PDF viewer can cut and paste the text properly, because it now knows that character code 1 is a bullet point (names like /bullet are predefined in the *Adobe Glyph List*). It makes no difference to the display of the PDF.

Example 6-1. A font encoding for a font with the bullet point added

```
25 0 obj
<< /Type /Font
   /Subtype /Type1
   /Encoding 23 0 R Reference to the encoding dictionary
   /BaseFont /Symbol
   /ToUnicode 24 0 R Instructions for conversion to Unicode
>>
endobj

23 0 obj Encoding dictionary
<< /Type /Encoding
   /BaseEncoding /WinAnsiEncoding The base encoding
   /Differences [ 1 /bullet ] The differences
```

```
>>
endobj
```

Embedding a Font

When creating a PDF file, the fonts must be *embedded*, so that the glyph descriptions and encodings are available to the program showing the PDF or processing it in other ways. To embed a font:

1. Various details from the font file are extracted—a process that varies depending upon the font format in question. These details (metrics, encodings etc.) are used to fill out a font dictionary, the font metrics, and the font encoding dictionary.

2. These details can now be stripped from the font file in question, if that is allowed by the font format, leaving just the glyph descriptions—all this information is now in the font dictionary. This reduces the size of the embedded font.

3. The font may be *subsetted*, removing whole glyph descriptions, reducing the font file to one which holds only the characters which are actually used. For example, a font only used for the title of a document may only actually use ten characters. Depending on the font format, the encoding may have to be altered to place all these characters in the first few character positions in the font so they are numbered 1,2,3.... Subset fonts are identified by a prefix formed of six uppercase letters followed by a +, such as RTFGRF+. This unique code is generated when the subset is created to allow different subsets to be distinguished from one another.

An example of an embedded font is given in Example 6-2.

Example 6-2. An embedded font, including encoding and font descriptor

```
9 0 obj
<</Type /Font
    /Subtype /TrueType  It's a TrueType font
    /BaseFont /GCCBBY+TT8Et00  Font is TT8Et00. GCCBBY+ prefix identifies as a subset font.
    /FontDescriptor 8 0 R
    /FirstChar 1  There are 41 characters in this font.
    /LastChar 41
    /Widths
      [603 603 603 603 603 603 603 603 603 603 603 603 603 603  The widths. It's a fixed-width font.
       603 603 603 603 603 603 603 603 603 603 603 603 603 603
       603 603 603 603 603 603 603 603 603 603 603 603 603]
    /Encoding 14 0 R
>>

14 0 obj  The font encoding
<< /Type /Encoding
    /BaseEncoding /WinAnsiEncoding  The base encoding
    /Differences  The changes. In this case, it's a subset font with the characters at position 1 onward.
      [1 /w /i /d /g /e /t /s /T /h /space /r /u /l /a /x /bracketleft
       /underscore /J /o /n /S /m /quotesingle /A /p /c /bracketright
       /one /colon /braceleft /b /k /braceright /v /period /parenleft
       /two /parenright /asterisk /y /P]
```

```
>>
endobj

8 0 obj  The font descriptor, giving the remaining metrics.
<< /Type /FontDescriptor
   /FontName /GCCBBY+TT8Et00
   /FontBBox [0 -205 602 770]
   /Flags 4
   /Ascent 770
   /CapHeight 770
   /Descent -205
   /ItalicAngle 0
   /StemV 90
   /MissingWidth 602
   /FontFile2 12 0 R  The actual font file, here in TrueType format.
>>
endobj
```

The details of the actual font formats (Type1, TrueType etc.) are not discussed here—in fact, they are not discussed in the PDF Standard either, but by external documents from the providers of those font formats.

Extracting Text from a Document

It is customary to include enough information in a file's font dictionaries to allow the actual character identities (rather than just the glyphs) to be retrieved. This is important to allow users to search and copy text from PDF viewing applications like Adobe Reader. In can also be used, in a more limited capacity, to allow edits to be made to the textual content of a document.

There are two mechanisms for this: the /Encoding entry in the font (which maps character codes to Adobe Glyph List entries like /bullet), and a more modern mechanism, the /ToUnicode entry which provides a program in a language defined by Adobe which maps character codes directly to Unicode entities. Here is an example of a /ToUnicode program for a font containing the single character U+2022 (a bullet point) with character code 1:

```
23 0 obj
<< /Length 317 >>
stream
/CIDInit /ProcSet findresource begin 12 dict begin begincmap /CIDSystemInfo <<
/Registry (Symbol+0) /Ordering (T1UV) /Supplement 0 >> def
/CMapName /Symbol+0 def
1 begincodespacerange <01> <01> endcodespacerange
1 beginbfrange
<01> <01> <2022>  Maps character code 1 to Unicode U+2022, the bullet point.
endbfrange
endcmap CMapName currentdict /CMap defineresource pop end end
endstream
endobj
```

Another hardship in the extraction of text is reconstructing the text operators within the content stream. Operators may split up the text for kerning or justification, and hyphenation at the end of lines can interrupt the stream of characters. Indeed, it is even possible that the text operators may be out of order. Usually, though, a good reconstruction of text may be produced from most modern files.

Resources

As well as the PDF Standard, there are a number of other documents which provide further detail on the topics discussed in this chapter:

- Unicode is described fully in The Unicode Standard, Version 5.0, published by The Unicode Consortium. A more digestible introduction is O'Reilly's own Unicode Explained by Jukka K. Korpela.
- Fonts and Encodings by Yannis Haralambous (O'Reilly) explains the various font formats used by PDF.
- The Adobe Font and Type Technology Center (*http://www.adobe.com/devnet/open type.html*) is a collection of historic and current documents for the various font formats and encoding systems, including pre-Unicode methods for encoding foreign languages.

CHAPTER 7

Document Metadata and Navigation

In this chapter, we discuss four topics related not to the visual appearance of a PDF document, but to the ancillary data which may also be included for interactive, onscreen use of documents, and the metadata used to carry extra information with a document for use by programs in a PDF workflow.

Destinations
> Data structures defining a position within a file. They can be used to specify where a *bookmark* or *hyperlink* points to. Bookmarks (properly called the *document outline*) are used as a table of contents for the document.

XML Metadata
> A stream containing an XML file in a specified format, containing some of the same metadata as the document information dictionary, together with additional fields.

File Attachments
> Allow whole files to be encapsulated in a document, much like an email attachment.

Annotations
> Allow text and graphics to be applied on top of a PDF page, separate from the main page content, for display by onscreen readers. One particular kind of annotation is the *hyperlink*, which allows a user to click somewhere on a page and be redirected to a destination elsewhere in the file.

Bookmarks and Destinations

A document's *bookmarks* (properly called the *document outline*) are a tree of entries (typically titles of chapters, sections, paragraphs etc.) which can be clicked on in a PDF viewer to move around the document. Each entry has some text and a *destination* describing where it links to.

Destinations

A destination defines a place in a PDF file, consisting of the page number, position within that page, and magnification to use when viewing that page. Destinations may be defined explicitly (as we will do for simplicity) or referenced by a name and looked up in a document-wide *name tree* listing all destinations. The bookmarks are typically displayed alongside the document in a PDF viewer.

Destinations are defined using an array object, with the contents depending upon the kind of destination. Destination syntax is summarized in Table 7-1.

Table 7-1. Syntax for destinations. "page" is an indirect reference to a page object. Destination positions are relative to the crop box (or the media box if there is no crop box) unless otherwise specified.

Array	Description
[*page* /Fit]	Display the page at a scale which just fits the whole page in the window both horizontally and vertically.
[*page* /FitH *top*]	Display the page with the vertical coordinate *top* at the top edge of the window, and the magnification set to fit the document horizontally.
[*page* /FitV *left*]	Display the page with the horizontal coordinate *left* at the left edge of the window, and the magnification set to fit the document vertically.
[*page* /XYZ *left top zoom*]	Display the page with (*left, top*) at the upper-left corner of the window and the page magnified by factor *zoom*. A null value for any parameter indicates no change.
[*page* /FitR *left bottom right top*]	Display the page zoomed to show the rectangle specified by *left, bottom, right,* and *top*.
[*page* /FitB]	Display the page like /Fit, but use the bounding box of the page's contents, rather than the crop box.
[*page* /FitBH *top*]	Display the page like /FitH, but use the bounding box of the page's contents, rather than the crop box.
[*page* /FitBV *left*]	Display the page like /FitV, but use the bounding box of the page's contents, rather than the crop box.

The Document Outline (Bookmarks)

The document outline consists of a tree of outline entries defined by an *outline dictionary* and a number of *outline item dictionaries*. The outline dictionary is pointed to by the /Outlines entry in the document catalog. The subentries (children) for an entry may be shown by default (*open*) or concealed by default and only revealed by clicking (*closed*). The outline dictionaries are summarized in Tables 7-2 and 7-3.

Table 7-2. Entries in an outline dictionary

Key	Value type	Value
/Type	name	If present, must be /Outlines.
/First	indirect reference to dictionary	An outline item dictionary for the first top-level item in the document outline. Required if any document outline entries present.
/Last	indirect reference to dictionary	An outline item dictionary for the last top-level item in the document outline. Required if any document outline entries present.
/Count	integer	The total number of open outline entries in all parts of the outline. May be omitted if no open entries.

*Table 7-3. Entries in an outline item dictionary *denotes a required entry*

Key	Value type	Value
/Title*	text string	Text to be displayed for this entry.
/Parent*	indirect reference to dictionary	Pointer to the parent of this item in the outline tree. Either another outline item dictionary or the top-level outline dictionary.
/Prev	indirect reference to dictionary	Pointer to the previous item at this level, if there is one.
/Next	indirect reference to dictionary	Pointer to the next item at this level, if there is one.
/First	indirect reference to dictionary	Pointer to the first child item of this entry, if it has one.
/Last	indirect reference to dictionary	Pointer to the last child item of this entry, if it has one.
/Count	integer	The number of open entries below this one, if this entry is open. If closed, a negative integer whose absolute value is the number of descendants which would be revealed if this item were to be opened by the user.
/Dest	name, string or array	The destination. Arrays are destinations, names are references to entries in the /Dests entry in the document catalog, strings are references to entries in the /Dests entry in the document's name dictionary.

Building an example

Consider a file with three pages. We wish to build the following hierarchy:

> Part 1 *(points to page one)*
>> Part 1A *(points to page two)*
>> Part 1B *(points to page three)*

The resultant code is shown in Example 7-1. The page objects in this document have object numbers 3, 5, and 7 for pages one, two and three respectively. Object 12 is the document catalog. Object 11 is the document outline dictionary, and objects 8, 9, and 10 are document outline item dictionaries.

Example 7-1. An example document outline

```
8 0 obj
<< /Parent 10 0 R /Title (Part 1B) /Dest [ 7 0 R /Fit ] /Prev 9 0 R >>
endobj
9 0 obj
<< /Parent 10 0 R /Title (Part 1A) /Dest [ 5 0 R /Fit ] /Next 8 0 R >>
endobj
10 0 obj
<< /Parent 11 0 R /First 9 0 R /Dest [ 3 0 R /Fit ] /Title (Part 1) /Last 8 0 R >>
endobj
11 0 obj
<< /First 10 0 R /Last 10 0 R  >>
endobj
12 0 obj
<< /Outlines 11 0 R /Pages 1 0 R /Type /Catalog >>
```

Adobe Reader displays the document and its outline as shown in Figure 7-1.

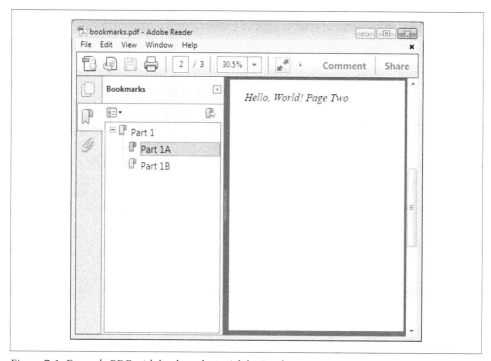

Figure 7-1. Example PDF with bookmarks in Adobe Reader

XML Metadata

Starting with PDF 1.4, *metadata streams* can be used to attach XML metadata to the whole document, or to individual elements within it. Document level metadata streams extend and supersede the document information dictionary (which is almost always included for compatibility with older PDF programs).

The metadata is stored uncompressed and (typically) unencrypted, and in such a way that external tools which don't know about PDF can find it within a PDF file easily.

The XML uses markup defined by the Extensible Metadata Platform (XMP) which is described in Adobe's *XMP: Extensible Metadata Platform*, and in ISO 16684-1. This format includes a method of embedding the metadata in other formats (e.g., PDF) in a platform-independent way so that programs which cannot understand the enclosing format can still extract the XMP data. Full details of the XMP Format are on Adobe's website (*http://www.adobe.com/products/xmp/*).

Example XMP metadata is shown in Example 7-2. You can see some of the familiar entries from the document information dictionary. Note also the sequence /Type / Metadata /Subtype /XML which identifies this stream as XMP metadata. A metadata stream is added to a document by using the /Metadata entry in the document catalog.

Example 7-2. XML Metadata for the ISO PDF Format reference manual PDF. The ↵ symbol is used to indicate a line which continues without a carriage return. The ␣ symbol is used to represent a space character.

```
4884␣0␣obj<</Length␣3508/Type/Metadata/Subtype/XML>>stream
<?xpacket␣begin='ï»¿'␣id='W5MOMpCehiHzreSzNTczkc9d'?>
<?adobe-xap-filters␣esc="CRLF"?>
<x:xmpmeta␣xmlns:x='adobe:ns:meta/'␣x:xmptk='XMP␣toolkit␣2.9.1-14,␣framework␣1.6'>
<rdf:RDF␣xmlns:rdf='http://www.w3.org/1999/02/22-rdf-syntax-ns#'␣↵
xmlns:iX='http://ns.adobe.com/iX/1.0/'>
<rdf:Description␣rdf:about='uuid:b8659d3a-369e-11d9-b951-000393c97fd8'␣↵
␣xmlns:pdf='http://ns.adobe.com/pdf/1.3/'␣↵
␣pdf:Producer='Acrobat␣Distiller␣6.0.1␣for␣Macintosh'>↵
</rdf:Description>
<rdf:Description␣rdf:about='uuid:b8659d3a-369e-11d9-b951-000393c97fd8'␣↵
␣xmlns:xap='http://ns.adobe.com/xap/1.0/'␣↵
␣xap:CreateDate='2004-11-14T08:41:16Z'␣↵
␣xap:ModifyDate='2004-11-14T16:38:50-08:00'␣↵
␣xap:CreatorTool='FrameMaker␣7.0'␣↵
␣xap:MetadataDate='2004-11-14T16:38:50-08:00'>↵
</rdf:Description>
<rdf:Description␣rdf:about='uuid:b8659d3a-369e-11d9-b951-000393c97fd8'␣↵
␣xmlns:xapMM='http://ns.adobe.com/xap/1.0/mm/'␣↵
␣xapMM:DocumentID='uuid:919b9378-369c-11d9-a2b5-000393c97fd8'/>
<rdf:Description␣rdf:about='uuid:b8659d3a-369e-11d9-b951-000393c97fd8'␣↵
␣xmlns:dc='http://purl.org/dc/elements/1.1/'␣↵
␣dc:format='application/pdf'>↵
<dc:description><rdf:Alt>↵
<rdf:li␣xml:lang='x-default'>␣Adobe␣Portable␣Document␣Format␣(PDF)␣</rdf:li>↵
</rdf:Alt></dc:description>␣↵
```

```
<dc:creator>_<rdf:Seq>_<rdf:li>↵
Adobe_Systems_Incorporated_</rdf:li>_</rdf:Seq>_</dc:creator>↵
<dc:title>_<rdf:Alt>↵
<rdf:li_xml:lang='x-default'>PDF_Reference,_version_1.6_</rdf:li>_</rdf:Alt>↵
</dc:title></rdf:Description>↵
</rdf:RDF>
</x:xmpmeta>
```
(Many more lines of padding)
```
<?xpacket_end='w'?>
endstream
endobj
```

Annotations and Hyperlinks

Annotations are used in PDF to add comments or interactive elements outside of the page content itself. Each viewer application (for example Adobe Reader or Mac OS X Preview) may display these annotations in a different way, even changing between software versions, so the exact visual effect cannot be relied upon. The annotations do not typically affect the printed output.

One or more annotations may be associated with each page using an array under the entry /Annots in the page dictionary. Each annotation is a dictionary. The more important entries are described in Table 7-4. Each type of annotation has additional entries in this dictionary.

*Table 7-4. Entries in an annotation dictionary (*denotes required entry)*

Key	Value type	Value
/Type	name	If present, must be /Annot.
/Subtype*	name	The type of this annotation.
/Rect*	rectangle	The location and size of the annotation in default user space units.
/Contents	text string	The textual content of this annotation, or if none, an alternate human-readable description.

We'll look at two kinds of annotations: *text annotations* which can be used to add comments, and *link annotations* which are used to make hyperlinks within a document. There are many other types for drawing on the document, highlighting text and adding printer's marks. In "File Attachments" on page 96, we use *file attachment annotations* to add attachments to individual pages.

First, a text annotation. Here, the /Subtype is /Text. The code is shown in Example 7-3. We set the extra annotation dictionary entry /Open to true to indicate the note will be visible when the document is opened. The background color is set to White with the /C entry.

Example 7-3. A Text annotation

```
6 0 obj
<<
  /Subtype /Text
  /Open true
  /Contents (An example text annotation)
  /Type /Annot
  /Rect [400 100 500 200]
  /C [1 1 1] RGB (1, 1, 1) i.e., White
>>
```

/Annots [6 0 R] *Extra entry in page dictionary*

The result in Adobe Reader is shown in Figure 7-2. Note that Adobe Reader ignores the /Rect entry here—other viewers may use it.

Figure 7-2. Example PDF with text annotation on page 1 in Adobe Reader

Now, let's try a link annotation, to build a hyperlink from page one to page three. A link annotation has subtype /Link and a /Dest entry giving the destination (described in "Destinations" on page 90). The /Rect entry defines the area of the hyperlink.

The code is shown in Example 7-4.

Example 7-4. A link annotation

```
6 0 obj
<<
  /Subtype /Link
  /Dest [4 0 R /Fit]
  /Type /Annot
  /Rect [45 760 260 800]
>>
```

/Annots [6 0 R] *Extra entry in page dictionary*

The result in Adobe Reader is shown in Figure 7-3.

Different border styles may be used, including ones to make the link rectangle invisible.

Figure 7-3. Example PDF with a link annotation on page 1 in Adobe Reader

File Attachments

An attachment is a way of including one or more files (of any type) within a PDF document. Files may be attached to the document as a whole, or to individual pages. Typically, the PDF viewer will display a list of any attachments, allowing the user to open or save them. This facility could be used, for example, to bundle example resources along with a PDF of a slide-show presentation.

The embedded file itself is simply included in a stream object, with `/Type /Embedded File` as an additional entry in the stream dictionary. The code for a sample embedded file is shown in Example 7-5.

Example 7-5. An embedded file

```
8 0 obj
<< /Type /EmbeddedFile /Length 35 >>
stream
This is a text file attachment...


endstream
endobj
```

The embedded file stream is referenced in two quite different ways: one for attachments to the whole document, another for attachments to particular pages.

To attach to the whole document, an `/EmbeddedFiles` entry is included in the name dictionary referenced by the `/Names` entry in the document catalog. The code is shown in Example 7-6.

Example 7-6. PDF code for an attachment at the document level. The embedded file is object 8 (see Example 7-5).

```
9 0 obj
<< /Names
      << /EmbeddedFiles
        << /Names
            [ (attachment.txt) << /EF << /F 8 0 R >> /F (attachment.txt) /Type /F >> ] >>
      >>
   /Pages 1 0 R
   /Type /Catalog >>
endobj
```

To attach to a single page, a special kind of annotation is used, listed as usual in the `/Annots` dictionary in the page dictionary. The code is shown in Example 7-7.

Example 7-7. PDF code for an attachment to a particular page. The embedded file is object 8 (see Example 7-5).

```
9 0 obj
<<
  /Type /Page

  (Other dictionary entries as usual)

  /Annots
    [ << /FS << /EF << /F 8 0 R >> /F (attachment.txt) /Type /F >>
        /Subtype /FileAttachment
        /Contents (attachment.txt)
        /Rect [ 18 796.88976378 45 823.88976378 ]
    >> ]
```

```
>>
endobj
```

Adobe Reader's display of the attachment in a sidebar is shown in Figure 7-4.

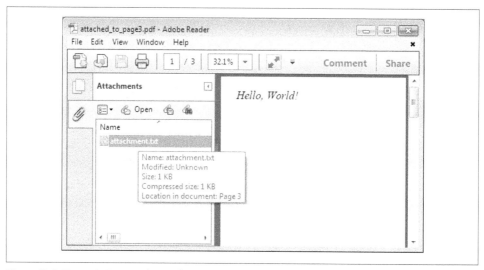

Figure 7-4. Example PDF with attachment on page three in Adobe Reader

CHAPTER 8

Encrypted Documents

PDF documents can be encrypted using a variety of industry-standard schemes which have increased in complexity and security over the years, starting with PDF version 1.1. The PDF standard provides, in addition, a general mechanism for encapsulating third-party encryption and security policies.

Encryption applies, with a few exceptions, to streams and strings in the file, but does not encrypt numbers or other PDF data types, nor does it encrypt the file as a whole. Thus, the document's object structure remains visible to applications without the need for decryption, but the substantive content of the document is safeguarded.

The more modern PDF encryption methods allow the file's XMP metadata stream ("XML Metadata" on page 93) to be left unencrypted so it may be extracted and read by programs which don't know how to open encrypted PDF files, or if the password is not known.

Introduction

Due to the complexity of encrypted documents, it isn't possible to manually build an example (as we have in other chapters), but we can use *pdftk* to process our standard *hello.pdf* file into an encrypted one, *encypted.pdf*:

```
pdftk hello.pdf output encrypted.pdf encrypt_40bit owner_pw fred
```

This creates the output file *encrypted.pdf* using the 40-bit RC4 method with an owner password of "fred". The *owner password* is the master password for the file. Someone who has it can do anything with the file, including re-encrypting it or changing the security settings. The *user password* allows the user to perform certain actions (view the document, print the document etc.) defined by the owner when the file was encrypted.

In our example, we're using a blank user password, which is very common. This means the file opens right away in a PDF viewer, without any password being entered. We've banned the user from doing anything other than viewing the file (see "Encryption and Decryption" on page 113 for details of the *pdftk* syntax for permissions and different encryption types).

When the file is opened in Adobe Reader, the only noticeable change is that (SECURED) is appended to the window's title bar. By opening the File...Properties window, and choosing the Security tab, the security properties can be viewed—see Figure 8-1. A more technically-minded display is obtained by clicking on the Show Details... button to bring up the window shown in Figure 8-2.

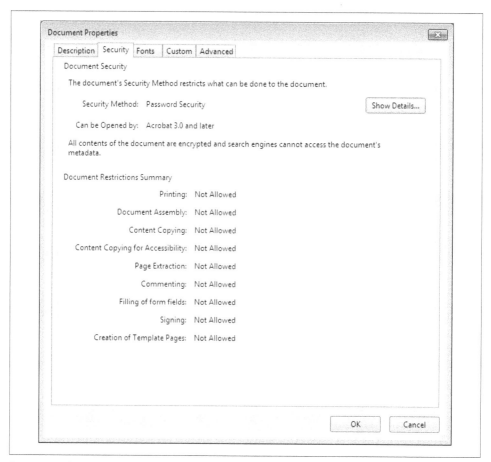

Figure 8-1. Security properties display in Adobe Reader for encrypted.pdf

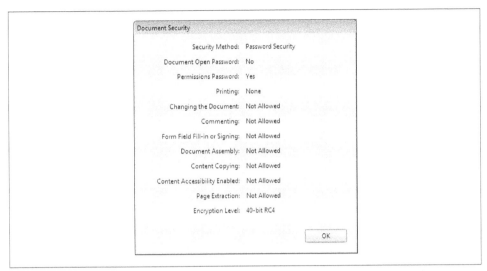

Figure 8-2. Security properties further detail display in Adobe Reader for encrypted.pdf

If using a program which can edit PDF files, such as Adobe Acrobat, the user will the prompted for the owner password upon attempting any editing operation not allowed by the permissions, as shown in Figure 8-3.

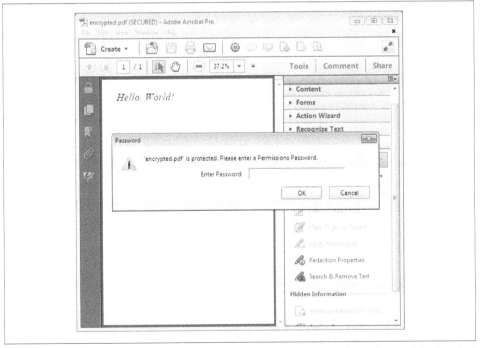

Figure 8-3. Entering the owner password in a program capable of PDF editing (here, Adobe Acrobat)

A similar dialog is presented upon opening the file if the document has a non-blank user password, as shown in Figure 8-4. If the password is not known, the file cannot be opened, even for viewing.

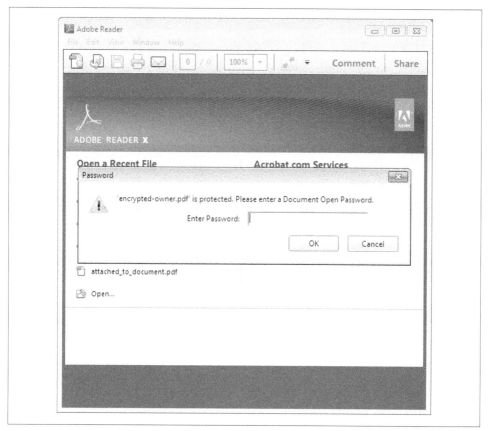

Figure 8-4. Opening a file with a non-blank user password in Adobe Reader

Example 8-1 shows the content of our new file. See if you can spot the differences from the standard *hello.pdf* file in Example 2-2.

Example 8-1. An encrypted file

```
%PDF-1.1
%âãÏÓ
1 0 obj
<< /Kids [2 0 R] /Type /Pages /Count 1 >>
endobj
3 0 obj
<< /Length 72 >>
stream
(72 bytes of encrypted data)
endstream
```

```
endobj
2 0 obj
<<
  /Rotate 0
  /Parent 1 0 R
  /Resources
  <<
    /Font
      <<
        /F0
          <<
            /BaseFont /Times-Italic
            /Subtype /Type1
            /Type /Font
          >>
      >>
  >>
  /MediaBox [0.000000 0.000000 595.275590551 841.88976378]
  /Type /Page
  /Contents [3 0 R]
>>
endobj
4 0 obj
<< /Pages 1 0 R /Type /Catalog >>
endobj
5 0 obj  The encryption dictionary
<<
  /R 2
  /P -64
  /O (ífff÷ÚÉMº]Òq)È¢ÏºA»fgygy^ÏynÔZ¾gtëÙ)
  /Filter /Standard
  /V 1
  /U (gdË^Wîg:lÆr({M8®qµG9Tæ$YTscåGùLÂÐþ¬)
>>
endobj xref
0 6
0000000000 65535 f
0000000015 00000 n
0000000199 00000 n
0000000074 00000 n
0000000427 00000 n
0000000478 00000 n
trailer
<<
  /Encrypt 5 0 R  Reference to encryption dictionary at object 5
  /Root 4 0 R
  /Size 6
  /ID [<a7d625071f5b223d97922e9e6c3fff23><e546c20487a77c4156083bf56f69bb4d>]
>>
startxref
617
%%EOF
```

The Encryption Dictionary

Look again at Example 8-1. An encryption dictionary has been included (object 5) and referenced by the /Encrypt entry in the trailer dictionary. This encryption dictionary contains, in this instance:

- The /R and /V entries which, together, define which encryption algorithms are to be used.
- The /P entry, which is a bitfield indicating the permissions (view, print etc.) which are attached to the use of the user password.
- The /O and /U entries which are used to verify the owner and user passwords respectively.
- The /Filter entry which is /Standard for Adobe security methods.

Standard encryption methods provided are:

40-bit RC4 (PDF 1.1)
128-bit RC4 (PDF 1.4)
128-bit AES Encryption (PDF 1.5)
256-bit AES Encryption (PDF 1.7 ExtensionLevel 3)

The permissions bitfield for 40-bit RC4 (the first method to be introduced) allows for a /P entry allowing a combination of printing, modification of the document, extraction of text and graphics, and annotation. The 128-bit RC4 and later methods allow more permission options.

The permissions are described in prose by the ISO standard and so the consistency of their implementation by different PDF processing programs cannot be relied upon.

Reading Encrypted Documents

Any encrypted file may be read as usual, and parsed into an object graph, without regard to its encryption. We can then inspect it for encryption by checking for the existence of an /Encrypt entry in the trailer dictionary. Then, we try to decrypt the file using the blank user password:

1. The contents of the encryption dictionary are read, and the encryption type determined.
2. The user password is authenticated (it is processed using a one-way algorithm, and compared with the /U entry in the encryption dictionary).
3. Using a further algorithm, an encryption key is calculated.
4. This key is used to decrypt each stream and string in the file. This can be done all at once or, more efficiently, only when an object is actually needed.
5. The permissions are read, and enforced in any further operations done on the file.

The actual algorithm used for each step depends upon the kind of encryption in use. The same process is used if the user password is non-blank, using the password entered by the user instead.

To decrypt using the owner password, a similar process is followed, except that the permissions need not be applied. If the file is opened with the user password and later, the owner password is entered, the permissions may be relaxed.

Writing Encrypted Documents

To write a parsed PDF to a file with encryption:

1. The /U and /O entries are calculated based a one-way algorithm combining the owner and user passwords.
2. The rest of the entries in the encryption dictionary are built, including the permissions, and the encryption dictionary is added to the trailer dictionary.
3. Each string and stream in the file is encrypted using a key calculated from the encryption dictionary.
4. The PDF object graph is flattened to a file in the usual fashion.

Again, the actual algorithms involved at each stage vary with the encryption method in use.

Editing Encrypted Documents

If the permissions on a file allow it to be edited with just the user password, we must be able to write the modified file, still encrypted with the same owner and user password. However, the algorithms given above would require the owner password to be known to encrypt the file again for writing.

To solve this problem, the encryption parameters from the original reading of the file are retained, even though the encryption dictionary itself must be removed once the file is decrypted. The encryption dictionary (including the /O and /U entries) may therefore be reconstructed.

CHAPTER 9

Working with Pdftk

Pdftk is a multiplatform command-line tool built on the *iText* library (which is described in "iText for Java and C#" on page 116). It has facilities for merging, splitting, and stamping documents, and for setting and reading metadata.

Obtaining Pdftk

Pdftk is an open source program, licensed under the GPL. Binary packages for Microsoft Windows and Mac OS X, and source code for all platforms can be found at PDF Labs (*http://www.pdflabs.com/tools/pdftk-the-pdf-toolkit/*).

The creator of *pdftk*, Sid Steward, is also the author of O'Reilly's *PDF Hacks*—a collection of tools and tips for working with PDF.

Command Line Syntax

Pdftk has a somewhat unusual command-line interface, where elements often have to appear in a particular order. We can split them into four groups, in the order they are specified:

1. The input file or files, and possible input passwords.
2. The *operation* and any arguments it requires.
3. The output and any output passwords and permissions.
4. Sundry output and other options.

The full details can be found in the manual for *pdftk*—in this chapter, we give only the subset needed for our examples.

Merging Documents

To merge documents, we use the `cat` operation. This is the default operation, so we don't actually need to specify the `cat` keyword. For example, to merge the pages of three files into one, in order, we need:

```
pdftk file1.pdf file1.pdf file3.pdf output output.pdf
```

This writes a new file to *output.pdf* containing all the pages of *file1.pdf*, *file2.pdf*, and *file3.pdf*, in order. The output file may not be the same as any of the input files.

Pdftk allows us to choose which pages are taken from each document, and what the viewing rotation of each output page is. Such *page ranges* are used by listing them in order after the inputs. For example:

```
pdftk file1.pdf file2.pdf 1-5 even output out.pdf
```

takes pages one to five inclusive from *file1.pdf* and pages two, four, six... from *file2.pdf*.

Page ranges in pdftk

A page range contains up to five parts:

- The input PDF *handle*, e.g., **B**. This is discussed below.
- The beginning page number.
- Optionally a dash, followed by the ending page number.
- An optional qualifier (**even** or **odd**), which modifies the page range already given.
- The page rotation:
    - — **N** (set rotation to 0°)
    - — **E** (set rotation to 90°)
    - — **S** (set rotation to 180°)
    - — **W** (set rotation to 270°)
    - — **L** (rotate by -90°)
    - — **R** (rotate by +90°)
    - — **D** (rotate by +180°)

Either page number can be **end** to refer to the last page of a document. The beginning page number can be larger than the ending page number (the pages will be taken in reverse order).

For example:

- **3** (page three only)
- **1-6** (pages one to six only)
- **1,4,5-end** (page one, page four, and all pages from page five onwards)
- **end-1** (all pages in reverse order)

To include pages from a file at two or more distinct points in the output, we can associate *handles* with each file by writing, for example `A=input.pdf`, and refer to those handles when giving the page ranges.

- `A1 A B` The first page of document `A` (duplicated as a cover page), then the whole of documents `A` and `B`.
- `A4-50oddD` Odd pages of file labeled `A` between 4 and 50, rotated by 180°.

For example:

```
pdftk A=file.pdf B=file2.pdf A1 A B output out.pdf
```

What Happens when Files are Merged

To perform a simple merge of PDF files in the manner of *pdftk*, the following steps might be performed:

1. Read each file into memory and create a graph of PDF objects, possibly lazily (i.e., parsing objects on demand, since not all of them will be needed if only certain pages are included).
2. Renumber the objects in the object graphs so they are mutually exclusive i.e., 1...p, p+1...q, q+1...r etc.
3. Put all these PDF objects into a new object graph.
4. Create a new page tree, containing the required combination of page objects from the original files.
5. Create a new trailer dictionary and root object, linking to the new page tree.
6. Write the new document to a file.

A fully functioning merge would also need to:

- Trim references to pages no longer in the document due to the use of a page range. Were this not done, a single reference to a page which is not in the output can result in the inclusion of all of the objects from that page, bloating the output.
- Remove duplicate font definitions. Often, files to be merged come from the same source, and share content like fonts. These can be deduplicated to save space.
- Combine the other parts of the file—bookmarks, destinations, forms and so on. Generally speaking, data which is strictly per-page survives automatically, but document-wide data needs specific merging support.
- Making decisions on where to take metadata and PDF version numbers from (for example, using the highest PDF version number amongst the inputs and taking the metadata from the first given file).

Splitting Documents

To take a selection of pages from a document, we use the same syntax as for merging, because our operation is equivalent to merging just one file with a page range:

```
pdftk file1.pdf 2-20 output out.pdf
```

This writes pages 2-20 inclusive to the output file. *Pdftk* has a separate facility for splitting a file into individual pages and writing them all to disk at once, using the *burst* operation.

```
pdftk input.pdf burst
```

By default, this writes the pages to *pg_0001.pdf*, *pdf_0002.pdf* etc. To write them with differently-formatted names, an output string in the style of the built-in C function printf may be provided. For example:

```
pdftk input.pdf burst output page%03d.pdf
```

would create *page001.pdf*, *page002.pdf* etc.

The burst operation also writes the document's metadata to the file *doc-data.txt*. We consider this functionality in "Extracting and Setting Metadata" on page 111.

What Happens when Files are Split

In order to split a PDF into several parts of one or more pages each, a program such as *pdftk* would take the following steps:

1. Load and parse the input document into an object graph, possibly lazily (so that pages which aren't going to appear in any of the output don't have to be processed).
2. Create a new, empty PDF data structure for each new document. Create a new page tree for each page range, using the same object numbers as the existing document.
3. Copy all the objects from the input PDF into each output PDF.
4. Remove all objects not required in each PDF (i.e., ones which are no longer referenced).

To perform the last step correctly, it is important to process bookmarks, destinations, and other cross-page objects to remove references to pages which no longer appear in a given output file, since a single errant reference could result in a source file's whole object graph being included, even though none of it is required.

Stamps and Watermarks

A *stamp* is a PDF page placed over another so that the page contents are combined. A *watermark* (which *pdftk* calls a *background*) is the same, but the stamp is placed under the existing page contents. This doesn't work well if the pages of the input PDF have a colored background, since the watermark often won't show through.

With *pdftk*, this is achieved using the `stamp` and `watermark` operations, which place the stamp on (or under) all the pages in the given range. If the page sizes differ, the stamp is scaled to fit and centered.

For example:

```
pdftk file.pdf stamp stamp.pdf output output.pdf
```

How a Stamp Is Added

When a program like *pdftk* adds a stamp to an input PDF, the following steps must be taken:

1. Load and parse both files into PDF object graphs.
2. Rectify the object numbers in both PDFs so that they are mutually exclusive. The objects from the stamp PDF may now be added to the input PDF.
3. The page data for the stamp is appropriately scaled and centered with relation to the page size of each page in the source PDF.
4. The page data for the stamp is appended to the page data for source PDF on each page. Resources like fonts and images must all be renamed so as not to clash. Any unmatched stack operators (`q`/`Q`) must be matched up prior to adding the new data.
5. The PDF can now be written to the output file.

Extracting and Setting Metadata

Pdftk can extract a document's metadata (author, title etc.) to a text file, either in ASCII format (with non-ASCII characters encoded as XML-style numerical entities) or as Unicode UTF8. This is achieved with the `dump_data` or `dump_data_utf8` keywords. For example:

```
pdftk input.pdf dump_data output data.txt
```

writes the data in Example 9-1 to *data.txt*.

Example 9-1. Example output of pdftk dump_data operation (ellipses indicate where we have truncated the output for brevity)

```
InfoKey: Creator
InfoValue: XSL Formatter V4.3 R1 (4,3,2008,0424) for Linux
InfoKey: Title
InfoValue: PDF Explained
```

```
InfoKey: Producer
InfoValue: Antenna House PDF Output Library 2.6.0 (Linux)
InfoKey: ModDate
InfoValue: D:20110713115225-05'00'
InfoKey: CreationDate
InfoValue: D:20110713115225-05'00'
PdfID0: 57f4673abea4ca58a27e19bf1871dfa
PdfID1: 57f4673abea4ca58a27e19bf1871dfa
NumberOfPages: 90
...
BookmarkTitle: Table of Contents
BookmarkLevel: 1
BookmarkPageNumber: 5
BookmarkTitle: Preface
BookmarkLevel: 1
BookmarkPageNumber: 9
BookmarkTitle: Why Read This Book?
BookmarkLevel: 2
BookmarkPageNumber: 9
BookmarkTitle: Audience
BookmarkLevel: 2
BookmarkPageNumber: 9
...
PageLabelNewIndex: 1
PageLabelStart: 1
PageLabelNumStyle: DecimalArabicNumerals
PageLabelNewIndex: 5
PageLabelStart: 5
PageLabelNumStyle: LowercaseRomanNumerals
PageLabelNewIndex: 13
PageLabelStart: 1
PageLabelNumStyle: DecimalArabicNumerals
```

This data lists:

1. Values and keys from the *document information dictionary*
2. The number of pages in the document
3. The bookmark titles, levels, and destination pages
4. The page labels

The update_info operation can be used to perform the reverse: to set the information listed above. There is also a corresponding update_info_utf8 operation. For example, we can modify the *data.txt* file we created and then use update_info:

```
pdftk input.pdf update_info data.txt output output.pdf
```

File Attachments

PDF files can have attachments added at the document or page level. The technical foundations of PDF attachments are discussed in Chapter 7. To add an attachment at the file level:

```
pdftk input.pdf attach_files file1.xls file2.xls output output.pdf
```

The attachment is added to the end of the list of file-level attachments. To add an attachment at the page level, use the **to_page** keyword:

```
pdftk input.pdf attach_files file1.xls to_page 4 output output.pdf
```

To extract the attachments from a document, writing them to a given directory, we can use the **unpack_files** keyword:

```
pdftk input.pdf unpack_files output outputs/
```

This writes the attachments, under their original filenames, in the *outputs* directory.

Encryption and Decryption

Pdftk has facilities for reading encrypted files, and for encrypting the output file.

Decrypting Input Files

The **input_pw** keyword can be used to specify owner passwords for the input file(s). The passwords are associated with the inputs by using handles, as with page ranges. If no handles are given, the passwords are assumed to be given in the same order as the input files. If the user password is given instead, most *pdftk* features will not be available, because the PDF security model would prevent it.

For example, to merge two files which are encrypted, the passwords can be provided thus:

```
pdftk file1.pdf file2.pdf input_pw fred charles output out.pdf
```

Here, "**fred**" is the password for *file1.pdf*, "**charles**" the password for *file2.pdf*.

Encrypting the Output

Pdftk can encrypt the output using the 40-bit or 128-bit RC4 encryption methods using the **encrypt_40bit** and **encrypt_128bit** keywords. We can specify the owner and user passwords using the **owner_pw** and **user_pw** keywords. For example, to encrypt a file with 128-bit encryption using an owner password, but the blank user password:

```
pdftk input.pdf output output.pdf encrypt_128bit owner_pw fred
```

Notice we leave out the **user_pw** keyword to indicate a blank user password.

We have not yet specified the operations to be allowed when the user password is entered. This can be done by using the `allow` keyword with one or more of the permissions (corresponding to those enumerated in Chapter 8):

```
Printing
DegradedPrinting
ModifyContents
Assembly
CopyContents
ScreenReaders
ModifyAnnotations
FillIn
AllFeatures (all of the above, plus top quality printing)
```

For example, to allow form filling, but nothing else:

```
pdftk input.pdf output output.pdf encrypt_128bit allow FillIn owner_pw fred
```

Compression

In order to view or edit page-level content like streams of graphics operators, it is necessary first to remove the compression used for the data stream. This can be achieved with the *pdftk* uncompress modifier:

```
pdftk compressed.pdf output uncompressed.pdf uncompress
```

The process can be reversed (following manual editing, for example) by using compress instead:

```
pdftk uncompressed.pdf output compressed.pdf compress
```

CHAPTER 10

PDF Software and Documentation

In this chapter we list and describe software for viewing, converting, editing, and programming with PDF files. We consider both open source software, and zero-cost commercial software where it is provided by Adobe or operating system manufacturers. There is a large variety of commercial software from third parties, which we do not discuss here.

We also list sources of further documentation and information.

PDF Viewers

The job of a PDF viewer is to:

- Display the graphical and textual content of the document.
- Allow the user to interact with the document using bookmarks and hyperlinks.
- Enable searching of the textual content, and extraction of text via cut and paste.

Not every viewer has all of these features. Due to the huge complexity of the PDF format and the formats it encapsulates (for example, fonts and images), performance can vary significantly—especially on files using more modern PDF features.

Adobe Reader

Adobe Reader is Adobe's own, free PDF viewer and the only one guaranteed to support most if not all of the features of PDF. It comes with a PDF plug-in for common web browsers, and is available for Microsoft Windows, Mac OS X, Linux, Solaris, Android, and iOS. It allows forms to be filled in and submitted electronically.

Adobe Reader can be found at Adobe's website (*http://get.adobe.com/reader/*).

Preview

Many Mac OS X users prefer the fast, simple PDF viewer Preview, provided with the operating system. It launches more quickly, and is smoother in use than Adobe Reader, with good support for searching and extracting text. Quick launching is especially important when the PDF viewer is loaded within a web browser window as a plug-in. Typically, Acrobat Reader is also installed for the occasions when Preview doesn't support a file (for example, a fillable form with JavaScript for a tax return).

In addition, Preview has limited (but increasing) editing capabilities, described in "Editing with Preview on Mac OS X" on page 119.

Xpdf

Xpdf is a small, fast, open source PDF viewer, running on virtually any Unix-like computer where The X Window System is available. Support for advanced PDF facilities is limited, but it is a highly reliable program for files within its capabilities.

Xpdf can be found at Foo Labs' website (*http://foolabs.com/xpdf*).

GSview

GSview is an open source PDF and PostScript viewer for Microsoft Windows and Unix. It is based on the venerable and highly reliable GhostScript PDF and PostScript interpreter.

GSview and GhostScript (which is required by GSview) can be downloaded from the GhostScript website (*http://pages.cs.wisc.edu/~ghost/*).

Software Libraries

Adobe provides its own commercially-licensed library for PDF manipulation, based on the same code as Acrobat itself. In this section, we consider popular open source alternatives.

In general, it's much easier to build libraries to write PDF files than to read them. To write a file, one need only understand the small subset of PDF required for a particular application (i.e., one compression mechanism, one font type etc.) and no complicated parsing mechanisms. To read a file, one must implement the whole standard.

iText for Java and C#

iText is a mature open source library for reading and writing PDF documents, and for making textual reports using high-level building blocks such as paragraphs, lists, tables, and images. It also has support for building bookmarks, hyperlinks, annotations, and JavaScript actions. Fillable forms can be constructed, and encrypted files are supported.

iText can be downloaded from the iText Software website (*http://itextpdf.com/*).

TCPDF for PHP

TCPDF is a pure PHP library for the generation of PDF reports, including text layout, tables, conversion of HTML, annotations, hyperlinks, and images. Web services can use TCPDF to build a document dynamically and serve it to a PDF viewer running within a web browser, or send it by email.

TCPDF can be downloaded, together with a wide range of examples from its website (*http://www.tcpdf.org/*).

Processing PDF with Perl

There are a large number of PDF libraries for reading, writing, and editing PDF files in Perl, some of which are highly mature, others less so. Documentation is often sparse, belying the extensive capabilities available.

As with all free Perl modules, the Comprehensive Perl Archive Network (*http://www.cpan.org/*) holds both source code and documentation.

PDF on Mac OS X

Apple's PDFKit provides a number of classes for use with Apple's supported programming languages (such as Objective C). These include:

- PDFView, an onscreen view on a PDF document.
- PDFDocument and PDFPage for document and page-level manipulation.
- PDFAnnotation, PDFAction, PDFOutline, and PDFSelection for interactive facilities.

Apple's built-in PDF viewer, Preview, is built on these libraries. The PDF Kit Libraries are documented in Apple's Mac OS X Developer Library (*http://developer.apple.com/*).

Converting Formats

Format conversions come in three categories:

- Converting to or from a similar, scalable vector format (e.g., PostScript or SVG). In this case, structural information is often preserved well.
- Converting from a PDF to a raster image, such as a PNG or TIFF.
- Converting from a raster image to a PDF, which often just involves simple encapsulation, especially in the case of formats PDF knows about, like JPEG.

PDF to PostScript and Back Again

The *pdf2ps* and *ps2pdf* command-line programs which ship with GhostScript can convert between PDF and PostScript. Sometimes this involves quite complicated and slow processing which may lead to larger file sizes or the loss of some constructs (for example, text being converted to outlines). PDF and PostScript are, after all, very different—despite a shared heritage.

ps2pdf and *pdf2ps* are available from the GhostScript home page (*http://pages.cs.wisc.edu/~ghost/*).

Rasterizing PDF to an Image

The *gs* program which comes with GhostScript can be used to render a PDF page to a raster image at a given resolution, suitable for printing or for onscreen use. This is the facility used by GSView to display PDF pages. This is achieved by specifying one of several special output devices which correspond to image file formats, such as PNG and TIFF.

gs is part of the GhostScript system, available from the GhostScript home page (*http://pages.cs.wisc.edu/~ghost/*).

Printing Files to PDF

Most modern word-processors have the facility to export as PDF, maintaining hyperlinks and building bookmarks for the table of contents. However, it is often necessary to produce PDF output from programs which do not have the facility to convert their native format to PDF. This can be achieved by the use of a printer driver which writes the PDF to a file, instead of printing it.

Mac OS X provides this facility natively, through the "Save as PDF" option in the print dialog.

On Unix platforms, this facility is provided by the open source CUPS-PDF backend to the CUPS printing system (*http://cups-pdf.de/*).

On Microsoft Windows, the open source PDFCreator printer driver (*http://sourceforge.net/projects/pdfcreator/*) achieves the same job. It uses GhostScript internally.

PDF Editors

PDFs were not originally intended to be edited significantly, but as a scalable, structured end-format for publishing. Thus, most editing software has restricted and specific editing functions such as merging files, adding annotations, filling in forms, or making small edits to page content.

In Chapter 9 we looked at *pdftk*, an open source program for command-line manipulation of PDF files. In this section, we list other ways of editing existing PDF files.

Adobe Acrobat

Adobe's own PDF editor, Acrobat (which costs several hundred dollars) has a wide range of functionality, over and above that of the free Adobe Reader. This includes:

- Printing to PDF, and conversion from PostScript to PDF.
- Conversion to and from Microsoft Word and Excel.
- Optical Character Recognition (OCR), producing a PDF file which looks exactly like the scanned document, but has searchable, editable text.
- Reordering, rotating, and editing pages and contents.
- Preflight and print publishing tools.
- Building PDF forms.
- Creating and validating PDF/A and PDF/X.
- Adding encryption and digital signatures.

There are many commercial third party plug-ins available for Adobe Acrobat, providing extra functionality.

Editing with Preview on Mac OS X

Preview, the standard PDF Viewing program on Mac OS X, also has editing facilites, which tend to be underused since they are not prominent in the interface.

Preview can annotate PDF documents, highlight and strike through text, crop pages, add text, add hyperlinks, delete and rearrange pages, and merge PDFs.

Preview deals with a wide range of documents, and manages to preserve functionality it doesn't understand when editing other aspects of the file.

PDF and Graphics Documentation

This book was written to fill a conspicuous gap in PDF literature. Here, we list other sources of information and documentation.

ISO 32000 and the PDF File Format

The *PDF Reference Manual* was published as a book until PDF version 1.6. Now, alas (but perhaps fittingly, given its subject matter), it is only available as a PDF document.

PDF version 1.7 was ratified as an ISO Standard in 2008 (Standard number ISO 32000-1:2008). The ISO charges almost 500 US Dollars for a PDF copy (by download, or on CD-ROM). Luckily, Adobe continues to provide the PDF Version 1.7 Reference electronically. This is an approved copy of ISO 32000-1:2008. In particular, the chapter, section, and subsection numbers are identical.

More recent Adobe extensions to PDF 1.7 are documented in *ExtensionLevel* documents, which do not form part of the ISO Standard, but would be expected to form part of a later, updated one.

Both Adobe's copy of ISO 32000-1:2008 and the ExtensionLevel documents can be downloaded from the Adobe Developer Connection Website (*http://www.adobe.com/devnet/pdf/pdf_reference.html*).

PDF Hacks

O'Reilly's other PDF title, *PDF Hacks* by Sid Steward, emphasizes practical solutions to a wide range of PDF problems. It includes 100 separate hacks to:

- Customize PDF viewers to make reading PDFs more comfortable.
- "Refry" huge PDF files into much smaller files.
- Create PDF files with a variety of tools on a number of platforms.
- Edit PDF text from the gVim text editor.
- Use familiar software to create PDFs with advanced navigation features.
- Build PDFs with sophisticated navigation and interactive features.
- Generate PDFs on the fly.
- Integrate PDF files with websites beyond a simple hyperlink.
- Collect data on a website with PDF forms.
- Index and compare PDF files.
- Convert incoming faxes to PDF.
- Write scripts that control Adobe Acrobat.

Related Topics

The PDF standard and this book make reference to (and sometimes assume knowledge of) the general area of computer graphics. The standard reference for these topics is *Computer Graphics Principles and Practice* (Foley et al., Addison-Wesley 1990). This book contains all the background on Bézier curves, transparency, affine transformations, and other topics needed to understand how to write PDF graphics streams.

A good reference for understanding the dictionaries, trees, and other data structures in PDF and why they were chosen is *Algorithms* (Cormen et al., MIT Press, 1990). Any similar book on algorithms should suffice.

Forums and Discussion

There are a number of places to discuss technical PDF topics:

- The Planet PDF Forums (*http://forum.planetpdf.com/*) are a popular venue for all sorts of technical and nontechnical PDF discussions.
- Adobe's Adobe Reader Forums (*http://forums.adobe.com/community/adobe_reader_forums/adobe_reader*) for technical support and discussion for Adobe Reader.
- The `comp.text.pdf` usenet newsgroup is a low traffic place for more technical discussions.

Adobe's Website Resources

There are two relevant sections of the Adobe website for those interested in the technical aspects of PDF:

- The PDF Technology Center (*http://www.adobe.com/devnet/pdf.html*) contains PDF reference documents.
- The Acrobat Developer Center (*http://www.adobe.com/devnet/acrobat.html*) has resources and documentation for writing Acrobat plug-ins, the FDF forms format, and a developer knowledge base.

Index

We'd like to hear your suggestions for improving our indexes. Send email to *index@oreilly.com*.

Type 1, 82
Type 3, 81, 82
font dictionary, 81
form XObject, 69

G

glyph, 81
graphics
    operators, 53
    state, 53
GSview, 116

H

header, 27
hexadecimal string, 32
hyperlink, 94

I

image, 70
incremental update, 3, 35
indirect reference, 33
integer, 31
ISO standardization of PDF, 3
iText, 116

K

kerning, 79

L

line endings, 30
linearization, 3, 36
link annotation, 94

M

media box, 42
merging PDF documents, 108
metadata, 7
    extracting and setting, 111
modification date, 45

N

name, 32
null value, 30

O

object stream, 35

OpenType font, 82
Optical Character Recognition (OCR), 11
optional content, 8
owner password, 99

P

page, 42
page description language, 1
page tree, 42
password, 99
path, 54
    filling, 58
    stroking, 54
    winding rule, 58
pattern, 66
PCL, 2
PDF
    advantages of, 2
    history of, 1
    ISO standardization of, 3
    process of reading, 37
    process of writing, 38
    versions of, 5
PDF viewer, 115
PDF/A, 4
PDF/X, 4
PDFKit, 117
pdftk, 13, 107
PostScript, 2, 118
Preview PDF viewer, 116

R

RC4 encryption, 104
reading a PDF file, 37
real number, 31

S

shading, 66
splitting a PDF document, 110
stamp, 111
stream, 33
string, 31
    hexadecimal, 32
    text string, 45
    Unicode, 45
subscript, 78
subsetting, 85
superscript, 78

T

tagged PDF, 9
TCPDF, 117
text, 73
    extraction of, 86
    rendering mode, 80
    showing, 76
text annotation, 94
text matrix, 75
text rise, 78
text space, 75
text state, 74
text string, 45
tiling pattern, 66
trailer, 29
trailer dictionary, 39
transparency, 66
TrueType font, 82
Type 1 font, 82
Type 3 font, 82

U

Unicode, 86
user password, 99
user space, 63

W

watermark, 111
word spacing, 76
writing a PDF file, 38

X

XML metadata, 93
XMP, 93
XObject, form, 69
XObject, image, 70
Xpdf, 116

Have it your way.

O'Reilly eBooks

- Lifetime access to the book when you buy through oreilly.com
- Provided in up to four DRM-free file formats, for use on the devices of your choice: PDF, .epub, Kindle-compatible .mobi, and Android .apk
- Fully searchable, with copy-and-paste and print functionality
- Alerts when files are updated with corrections and additions

oreilly.com/ebooks/

Safari Books Online

- Access the contents and quickly search over 7000 books on technology, business, and certification guides
- Learn from expert video tutorials, and explore thousands of hours of video on technology and design topics
- Download whole books or chapters in PDF format, at no extra cost, to print or read on the go
- Get early access to books as they're being written
- Interact directly with authors of upcoming books
- Save up to 35% on O'Reilly print books

See the complete Safari Library at safari.oreilly.com

Get even more for your money.

Join the O'Reilly Community, and register the O'Reilly books you own. It's free, and you'll get:

- $4.99 ebook upgrade offer
- 40% upgrade offer on O'Reilly print books
- Membership discounts on books and events
- Free lifetime updates to ebooks and videos
- Multiple ebook formats, DRM FREE
- Participation in the O'Reilly community
- Newsletters
- Account management
- 100% Satisfaction Guarantee

Signing up is easy:

1. **Go to: oreilly.com/go/register**
2. **Create an O'Reilly login.**
3. **Provide your address.**
4. **Register your books.**

Note: English-language books only

To order books online:
oreilly.com/store

For questions about products or an order:
orders@oreilly.com

To sign up to get topic-specific email announcements and/or news about upcoming books, conferences, special offers, and new technologies:
elists@oreilly.com

For technical questions about book content:
booktech@oreilly.com

To submit new book proposals to our editors:
proposals@oreilly.com

O'Reilly books are available in multiple DRM-free ebook formats. For more information:
oreilly.com/ebooks

O'REILLY®

Spreading the knowledge of innovators   oreilly.com